D1626539

The Pre-Emptive Empire

The Pre-Emptive Empire

A Guide to Bush's Kingdom

Saul Landau

Pluto Press

LONDON • STERLING, VIRGINIA

First published 2003 by Pluto Press
345 Archway Road, London N6 5AA
and 22883 Quicksilver Drive, Sterling, VA 20166–2012, USA

www.plutobooks.com

British Library Cataloguing in Publication Data
A catalogue record for this book is available from the British Library

ISBN 0 7453 2140 2 hardback

Library of Congress Cataloging in Publication Data
Landau, Saul.
  The pre-emptive empire : a guide to Bush's kingdom / Saul Landau.
    p. cm.
Includes bibliographical references and index.
  ISBN 0–7453–2140–2 (hardback)
  1. United States—Foreign relations—2001– 2. United States—Military
policy. 3. United States—Politics and government—2001– 4. Bush,
George W. (George Walker), 1946– 5. War on Terrorism, 2001– I. Title.
  E902.L36 2003
  973.931—dc21
                                                          2003011373

10   9   8   7   6   5   4   3   2   1

Designed and produced for Pluto Press by
Chase Publishing Services, Sidmouth, EX10 9QG, England
Typeset from disk by Stanford DTP Services, Towcester, England
Printed and bound in the United States of America by
Phoenix Color Corp.

Contents

Part V: Cuba—The Last Hold Out

Part VI: The Move to War

Acknowledgements

I owe a debt to my colleagues at the Institute for Policy Studies in Washington and the Transnational Institute in Amsterdam for having educated me and stimulated my brain for 30 plus years. They are extraordinarily wonderful people and places.

The atmosphere provided by the California State Polytechnic University, Pomona and especially by President Bob Suzuki, Dean Barbara Way and Vice-President Michael Berman allowed me the space and freedom to write—and do other things intellectual as well. My colleagues at Cal Poly also provided me with stimulating political conversation and support.

The gutsy Francisco Aruca inspired me to write about some of the themes in the book for his *Progreso Weekly* web site—a voice of reason from Cubans in Miami. *ZNET* and *Counterpunch*, outstanding web magazines, have published my essays and encouraged me to write.

Two people stand out as special in the production of this book. Farrah Hassen, my student assistant, critically read the essays, did valuable research and all the necessary detail work. She is the absolute best. Rebecca Switzer offered her critical eye and caught some of my errors in thinking, writing and formulating. She is a great editor and also a source of inspiration.

I owe all mistakes in the book to my own limitations and not to other people who tried their best to help me.

Foreword

George McGovern

Saul Landau has always been a passionate patriot of the highest order. In all the years I have known him as a friend and admired him as a literary and political analyst, he has consistently sought to identify those policies and priorities that would best serve the interests of both the American people and the world's citizens.

A fearless critic of policies that contradict the US's founding and enduring national ideals, he is an equally vigorous advocate of common sense reform in the liberal tradition of Tom Paine and Jefferson or the conservatism of a John Quincy Adams or an Edmund Burke. A steady stream of provocative essays, lectures, media programs, and films have poured from his independent and creative mind for many years. No one has ever experienced a conversation with Saul Landau without noticing his dancing eyes, his glad heart and his never failing search for the reality of things.

The Pre-emptive Empire embraces all of these qualities. You will read of his growing conviction that George W. Bush, a congenial young man and the son of a wealthy, somewhat aristocratic family, has been taken over by an extreme right-wing cabal far removed from the mainstream of American society. In the author's view, the advisers who now have the President's ear represent neither of America's two great political traditions—liberalism that traces its heritage to Jefferson, Lincoln, Wilson and Franklin Roosevelt, or the conservatism of Hamilton, Adams, Taft and Eisenhower.

Rather, writes Landau, the policies and priorities emanating from the Bush White House are the fruits of extremist, hard-line, rightist dreams—sometimes irresponsible dreams that neither Jefferson nor Hamilton, Roosevelt or Eisenhower, would recognize as sound public policy at home or abroad.

The author—a widely experienced student and observer of poor Third World countries—believes the globalization policies of the last two decades haven been especially harsh in their impact both on American workers and their counterparts in the developing world. American workers have lost their jobs as corporations seeking low-wage labor and no strict environmental requirements have moved their plants to Third World countries. But when Saul Landau went to Mexico to visit with the workers hired there by run-away American corporations, he found workers employed under miserable conditions and at ruinously low wages. Some of the factories were preparing to move to China where they would pay even lower wages to a newly converted peasant workforce.

A long-time student of US–Cuba relations and a frequent visitor to Cuba, the author discusses what he believes to be the irrational and self-defeating nature of the US government's policies toward Cuba since 1960.

The reader is going to enjoy the stimulating, alternative policies proposed in this book. Saul Landau has always approached every subject of interest with two questions: What is the problem? What is the solution? This book is faithful to that time-tested equation.

Introduction:
Before the Era of Insecurity

In this book, I offer extended journal excerpts as contemporary history. I chronicle and analyse some key events and ideas that have arisen in this watershed period of the US Empire, before and after the 9/11 attacks. By sharing with readers my immediate reflections, I hope to provide a prism through which readers can view the recent past as part of their present. I also refer to the more distant past as a constant reference point.

After 9/11, as much of the world recoiled in shock, the US media began to televise a stupefying loop of images of the infamous day, interrupted by information bites provided by the US government. It offered the most trite of historical contexts for the events. In the newspaper editorials and TV and radio commentaries, the pundits tended to suggest courses for immediate action as if terrorism had no antecedents. The President should immediately avenge the dirty deeds!

Few commented on the causes of the attacks or the significance of the President and Vice President going into hiding at that dramatic moment. Instead, TV news directors endlessly repeated the sci-fi-like pictures of the burning Tower One and the plane flying into Tower Two. Then came images of the Pentagon aflame. Citizens stared, mesmerized by the sight of the impossible, and shook their heads in disbelief.

TV directed the public to divide the images into good and evil. Rudolph Giuliani, the Mayor of New York, took charge as a hero at the site of the catastrophe as Bush began to emerge from his two-day trance.

For most of the country, the virtual had become the real. Yet, the mass media did nothing to channel the population toward dialogue, much less reflection on the events themselves. Instead, TV elicited sympathy for the dead, praise for the heroes and scorn for the villains. (Viewers saw the avengers and the rescuers as the good guys and the swarthy males wearing *kefiyas* on their heads as the black hats.) In this way our media (I include here White House and State Department press secretaries) would conduct the post-traumatic orchestra. Few commentators asked: what did these fiends want?

Some leftists talked conspiracy, including a role for the CIA and Israel's Mossad. I sighed in despair. I thought of the people I knew inside the national security gates of the US and British governments, the opportunists who didn't have the imagination to hatch such a diabolical plot but who after the events saw the inherent possibilities of expanding their own power and influence. Some of those scheming bureaucrats viewed 9/11 as the chance to adorn the most trivial of their departments' issues with the sacred drapes of 'national security,' which they quickly hung over the windows of routine policies and procedures. They also took advantage of the vacuum of oversight during the traumatic post-9/11 days. Who would monitor them while the President directed all government energy to meet the crisis?

A silent and unseen panic seemed to vibrate through the public, a kind of national anxiety attack encouraged by official pronouncements of impending danger. As the media predictably embellished all potentially bloody and explosive stories, the ambience of the heightened 'security' state reverberated through the halls of Congress.

Without significant debate, the members, more panicked than the public, passed the Uniting and Strengthening America by Providing Appropriate Tools Required to Intercept and Obstruct Terrorism Act (October 25, 2001), aka the USA Patriot Act, enabling non-elected officials to assume increased bureaucratic control through the tightening of immigration procedures, the legalization of intrusion into personal privacy, including the probing of social organizations and their bank accounts, and the invasion of telephone and computer messaging. Within months, bureaucracies had created their near perfect world, one of permanent emergency in which the CIA, FBI and the newly created Homeland Security Department could escalate their anxiety–security game.

Yes, real terrorists destroyed buildings and thousands of people, but the very agencies that failed to prevent the 9/11 acts successfully covered their intelligence lapse by evoking fear. The mysterious and evil Al-Qaeda plotters, government officials repeated, would return. The citizenry now had to contain a fear of epic proportions in addition to already mounting anxieties caused by economic recession, such as concerns over job and healthcare security. Then came the anthrax scare, which also baffled the FBI.[1]

In Washington DC, as veteran observers have learned, nothing succeeds like failure. Incompetent agencies, already unwieldy in size and with top-heavy hierarchies and inflated budgets, now possessed even larger budgets and were managed by the same lethargic, but more powerful, insiders. And the money, as all Washington insiders know, must get spent before the end of the fiscal year.

Most important, since Congress and the courts had agreed, the citizens could no longer claim certain inalienable rights. The media, which feeds anxiety to the public as its own means of reproducing itself, loved the emergency atmosphere, but appeared indifferent to the citizens' loss of rights.

Its message to the panicky public: 'You better watch TV or you might miss something vital in the daily hysteria about terrorism!' Security had become incompatible with liberty. But this conclusion did not make headlines.

The quotidian salvo of bloody and trivial stories makes concentration hard, the obvious obscure. Indeed, one can read daily newspapers from small towns or major metropolitan areas and watch and listen to the network and local news without ever hearing the obvious fact: a small group of fanatic Muslims successfully attacked the greatest empire in the history of the world.

But Americans presume they live in a republic. The dictionary defines 'republic' as the antonym of 'empire.' The imperial government availed itself of the confusion and offered a transcendent message to cover the fact that it no longer even wore republican clothes: revenge!

EMPIRE VERSUS REPUBLIC:
THE POLITICALLY UNCONSCIOUS AMERICAN

'The brilliance of the American political system for 200 years lies in its giving the rich a license to steal from the poor and making them think they voted for it.'—Gore Vidal at a 1995 Washington DC dinner party at Marcus Raskin's house

This book addresses the Empire in its most aggressive stage as it extends itself widely in the name of fighting terrorism and spreading democracy. It also focuses on the American public who have never thought of themselves as imperialists; nor have they acknowledged—except for an elite few—that they have benefited from their government's two centuries of expansionist policies. In 2003, as California's 34 million inhabitants wring their hands in despair over a $35 billion budget deficit,[2] hardly any of them know that in 2002 the economy generated by China's 1.2 plus billion people had finally equaled the size of California's.[3]

Likewise, despite an avalanche of daily statistics from the media, the informed citizen has difficulty getting a clear explanation about who gets what from the trillion plus dollars in the national budget. Yet, with the advent of Internet access, industrious researchers can discover in seconds that the filthy rich will get even filthier and richer when the President, selected by the Republican dominated Supreme Court, rams his ten-year $1.35 trillion tax-cut bill through Congress.[4]

If you listen to AM Talk Radio or glance at the headlines you will not get that story. Nor will reading the lead paragraphs or watching the anchors and reporters on the nightly news lead citizens to awareness. 'If it bleeds, it leads,' still dictates news priorities. When a rare piece of investigative reporting does appear, say unearthing a covert operation or a major business scandal, the reporter still must print the official or corporate denial in the second paragraph as if it has equal weight with the truth of the first paragraph.

When in the early 1980s reporters learned, for example, that the CIA had undertaken a covert action against the leftist Sandinista government of Nicaragua, they trumpeted that fact in headlines and lead graphs. But the second paragraph in their stories stated the predictable White House denial. An uninformed reader would have to make up his or her own mind: believe the journalist or the President. Why didn't the second paragraph simply begin with, 'As expected, the White House lied and tried to dissemble, but this newspaper has the facts. The United States government has decided to wage an illegal war to overthrow a left-wing government.'

Similarly, throughout the 1980s the CIA covertly armed, trained, financed and encouraged fanatical Muslims to destroy the communist government of Afghanistan, but neither Congress nor the media debated the worst case scenarios of providing those 'freedom fighters' with weapons of considerable destruction. The men the CIA lavishly supplied with arms, including Stinger surface-to-air missiles, hated not just communism, but western ideas and values, ones that date from even before the Reformation and Renaissance eras. Now the former 'freedom fighters' focus their ire on the American colossus.

The *secrecy about the very existence* of the American Empire stems from official denial. How many US presidents have used 'imperial' to describe the US system? They continue to speak of the Republic while they destroy its meaning in imperial adventures abroad or at home—carried out under the aegis of 'national security.'

When officials discuss the pledge of allegiance they fixate on the 'under God' phrase—does it violate the church–state separation?—not on 'to the Republic for which it stands.' For accuracy, that phrase should now read 'to the Republic for which it *used* to stand.'

THE NEW AXIOMS OF POWER

The media automatically accepts the axioms of American policy as the White House issues them. This becomes the foundation for subsequent dis- and mis-information. The cold war, like the Vietnam War and invasions of Grenada and Panama and the Iraq War campaign in 2002, was characterized by official lies. In the post-World War II development of the Cold War, dubious statements about the nature of the Soviet threat to invade Western Europe took on canonical stature. In fact, in the immediate post-World War II period the USSR had no food, boots for its army or railroad gauges that matched those of Eastern Europe, making supply of an invading army somewhat doubtful. Nevertheless, outrageous statements of Soviet aggressive intent became pillars of policy, as did the 2002 allegations that Iraq's Saddam Hussein constituted a threat to US security because he had accumulated weapons of mass destruction and intended to deliver them to his terrorist allies. If left unquestioned, big lies turn into axioms and then into destructive policy—cold war or hot war.

In tandem, an issue that continues to shape the security–insecurity themes of the world, the permanent Israeli–Palestinian crisis, focuses on Palestinian 'terrorism' and suicide bombing. Politicians and media moguls fear to proclaim the obvious: it's the occupation, stupid!

The media takes a Palestinian suicide bombing and not only distorts the meaning of the act, but terrifies the readers, listeners and viewers. The world becomes encapsulated in reports of Palestinian fanatics and then local serial killers on the loose (in October 2002, the number of people killed by the Washington sniper was lower than the average homicide rate for the area), or unrelated violence, followed by environmental—or 'natural'—catastrophes. The polar ice caps are melting along with the ice layers in the Andes and Mount Kilimanjaro. The seashore is rapidly receding and millions will lose their homes. Global warming may not affect you, if you're old, but your kids and grandchildren will suffer terribly.

Indeed, environmental disasters and the outbreaks of murderous madness may have increased, but as much as the daily information sources herald the importance of Nature's lurking perils, they devote little space or time to causation. The very production system we rely on might well turn into the destruction system for Nature.

The pressures of modern life increase obligations—'be all that you can be'—and may drive people mad; the very kind of culture that emanates from shopping, that creates the human and automobile traffic jams, urges ever more speed on people in work activity. 'God, it's taking forever to get on line,' as two seconds pass. What impact does such pressure exert on the brain?

HOW TO EXPLAIN EMPIRE TO CITIZENS OF A REPUBLIC?

History means the actual record of past events, not the display of some of its items stored in an attic that acquire importance only on special days. Like the word 'freedom' in the era of the expanding US Empire and the erosion of civil liberties, 'history' demands new explanations.

When, for example, President George W. Bush (43) explained the terrorists' motive for their fiendish deeds of 9/11—they hate us because we're free[5]—he omitted a few important facts as well as all analysis. But he's not exactly a detail kind of guy. If the 'they hate us because we're free' equation is sound, then the Attorney General John Ashcroft's trashing of civil liberties should free us from the evil-doers' hate.

The brevity of explanation and the paucity of facts given to the public and Congress about so-called national security and foreign policy issues compete only with the Orwellian logic employed in the terse briefings held by unelected 'security' officials.

Take policy relating to Cuba for example. The banalities and inconsistencies of US Cuba policy illustrate how a small gang of extreme right-wing anti-Castro Cubans control a piece of US foreign policy. The media has not examined the four-decade-old embargo and travel ban, but accepts them as somehow acceptable leftovers of cold war policy. Likewise, the media somehow excludes anti-Castro violence from its terrorist equation.

Similarly, the 'experts' on TV talk shows do not dramatize the absurdities of the 'free trade' order in the age of global warming, environmental degradation and rapidly growing poverty. Do they not see the screaming need for regulation? The mainstream media accept corporate globalization as the necessary engine of development for our time and use the euphemism 'trade' to cover all speculative investment. *New York Times* columnist Thomas Friedman's 1999 *The Lexus and the Olive Tree*[6] offers this rationalization in its most sophisticated and liberal form. But Third World facts belie Friedman's glib justification of globalization, which is the ultimate polarizing of the world's wealth. The exhaust fumes from the Lexus may well extinguish the olive tree, to extend his metaphor.

In the essays on Argentina and Mexico, I illustrate the disaster caused by the economic model imposed by the acronism experts. Under the IMF, World Bank, GATT, NAFTA, and WTO, the mavens have pushed their 'export' model down the throats of billions of people in Africa, Asia and Latin America. Despite riots, increased poverty, ecological disaster and demonstrated economic failure, the 'experts' insist on the correctness of their formula. As the former Brazilian president Medici said in 1971, after having applied an early version of the neo-liberal model to his country, 'Our model is very good for Brazil, but not so good for Brazilians.'[7]

HISTORY AS THE PRESENT

The relentless pursuit of justice remains the noble theme that has united different people and appears only in inchoate form in the established media. These journal entries try not to lose sight of the victims of Brazil's fascist generals or Augusto Pinochet's dictatorship in Chile from 1973 until 1990, or the plight of Mayan Indians in Chiapas; nor are they oblivious to the suffering of the blue- and white-collar workers.

So, the pre-9/11 world is well worth remembering. The US Empire began long before the World Trade Center collapsed. But in the twenty-first century, the American Empire can no longer maintain even a façade of compatibility with the foundations of its Republic. Americans will continue to demand accountability from those in power, just as they have in the past. Indeed, the anti-war demonstrations that occurred before the war in Iraq, the massive protests against corporate globalization and the solidarity shown with Palestinian people all indicate that some Americans (including Republicans and others who have not previously demonstrated) have begun to act to recapture the pillars of the Republic from the imperialists in power.

Part I

Leaving the Republic Behind

The following entries provide clues to help solve the puzzle of Empire.

WHO IS GEORGE W. BUSH AND
WHO MADE HIM PRESIDENT?*

During the 2000 pre-election debates my wife described George W. Bush as a dry drunk, an alcoholic who no longer drinks, but has not entered a recovery program to deal with the causes and consequences of his alcoholism. Drug addicts and alcoholics self-medicate to avoid the pains of maturing. Therefore, W, if my wife observed accurately, suffers from arrested development. I postulated that instead of submitting to serious rehabilitation, Bush attended some fundamentalist version of EST.[8]

His superficial veneer of certitude and self-assurance showed during campaign interviews and press conferences. After Bush used up the bromides his handlers had induced him to memorize as his standard retorts, he flashed that perplexed look, one that hinted at vulnerability and immaturity—the proverbial deer caught in the headlights.

His opponent, Al Gore, the Vice President, never materialized as an A-type contender. His 1993 book on the environment, *Earth in the Balance: Ecology and the Human Spirit*,[9] showed him as a man who had developed a well-reasoned albeit moderate approach to the polluters—that is, campaign contributors. But he didn't quite shed his enigmatic shell to project that trust-inducing Alpha male image that Americans seem to want at the helm.

The election campaign didn't tackle the big issues—national and world disparity of wealth, environmental decline, ongoing local wars, proliferation of weapons, endemic poverty and AIDS. Rather, managers in both parties focused their candidates' attentions on winning by any means necessary; thus, they presented the voters with a frivolous choice. Yes, Gore sounded more liberal, Bush more right-wing, but successive tides of money rolling into both electoral campaigns have steadily eroded the historic differences that distinguished the two parties. Democrats once stood for the workers and tenants; Republicans for bosses and landlords. But costs of winning office mounted, because candidates converted television into their stump. High corporate rollers then grabbed greater control of the outcome by contributing to both parties. Now, the primary process alone serves to weed out those who can't accumulate a sufficiently potent war chest or fail to convince pollsters of their viability.

---

* Originally appeared as a radio commentary on *Pacifica Network News* (Pacifica station) and later in the *Anderson Valley Advertiser*, November 22, 2000 (substantially revised for the book). Written two weeks after election day (November 5) while the media was still revealing voting irregularities. The *AVA* is a unique weekly newspaper published in Boonville, California (wherever that is) that prints local, national and international news and sells copies in bookstores and newsstands all over the world.

So, for a billion dollars mostly spent on TV spots we experienced what the *New York Times* columnist Maureen Dowd called a high school election.[10] No wonder those who planned to vote wanted this dull farce to end. Two mediocre men spending a billion dollars to repeat lines their handlers learned from focus groups!

The majority didn't vote. By not doing so, as always, they made a statement about their priorities. Voting for president doesn't compare to shopping or stressing out. Those who voted expressed a center-left-populist sentiment. Some 52 per cent of the voters who went to the polls chose Gore, Ralph Nader for the Green Party or Pat Buchanan for the Populist-Nativist Reform ticket. Bush received about 23 per cent of the eligible vote—hardly a mandate. That's the best conclusion I could draw from the sad event in which the rich and powerful select the two main candidates.

THE BUSHES AS PRIZZIS*

In the post-election period, irony has turned to farce. The world watched the ubiquitous preachers of American democracy, who have told everyone else how to run elections, follow the dubious wisdom of Joe Stalin: 'Those who cast votes decide nothing, those who count the votes decide everything.'

Daddy Bush (41) sips his martini while W guzzles his diet Pepsi. Celebration! The Bushies cut a few deals, negotiated some propitious pay-offs in Florida, some strategic Supreme Court appointments and, since the Democrats didn't resist against the Republicans' aggressive fraud, W slid into the presidency. The chosen son has no qualifications for the job—nor did his father or most of his predecessors for that matter—but the voting minority has long forgotten about things like criteria for top jobs.

A generation ago the New England patrician Bushes moved to cowboy country and apparently learned enough hybrid tricks to successfully filch the 2000 election. How about those Texas Prizzis? Recall in Richard Condon's *Prizzi's Honor*[11] how the Don, who has stolen billions and murdered countless people whom he named as 'enemies,' orders Charley, the hit man, to murder his lover. 'I love her,' protests Charley. 'She's a thief, she stole *our* money,' screams the Don.

---

* Originally appeared as a radio commentary on *Pacifica Network News* and later in the *Anderson Valley Advertiser*, January 3, 2001 (substantially revised for the book). Written shortly after the Supreme Court selected George W. Bush (5–4) as the 43rd President of the United States.

So, as the Florida election results came in—or were nullified—Don Preppy Georgio (41) gathered his Protestant primos to celebrate. 'Our family deserves this election,' he said. He instructed Dick Cheney to instruct his *spin dottores* to tell the media: 'Al Gore is trying to steal the election.' Never mind that Gore won the popular vote by half a million votes; that exit polls, which don't lie, showed Gore as the Florida winner; that thousands of Democratic voters of color encountered mysterious obstacles on their way to the voting booth or discovered that their names had been erased from the voter list. Republicans scoffed at other irregularities, like busloads of seniors of the anti-Castro persuasion showing up to vote at south Florida polling places—albeit they were Cuban citizens.

To help turn the outcome, the Prizzi Bushes found a Democratic Party 'traidore,' Miami's mayor, Alex Penelas, indignant over Bill Clinton's refusal to keep the little Cuban boy (Elian Gonzalez, more about him later) here in freedom. The acquiescence of this turncoat in stopping the Miami recount, busloads of Republican intimidators sent to Florida to scare the counters and a dozen or so Castro-hating gunsels helped stop a real counting of the votes.

The spinners told the media that they had played by the rules—referring to rules they had quickly invented after the election seemed to go the wrong way. Who believes in human vote counting, they asked, even though good old Texan law admits the good old human recount. In Miami, the incomplete count and recount appeared to favor Bush. But who knew what a detailed enumeration would yield? So, stressing loyalty, the Bush *familia* pressed the Supreme Court to decide. Daddy Bush knew he could count on this august body to devise a proper legal twist. Indeed, he must have chuckled when he read that his black robed buddies had solemnly declared (5–4)[12] that American democracy does not include vote counting. The unquestioning media responded predictably—without much skepticism—to the Bush display of power and class confidence. Bush won, the media declared. Gore waffled, then buckled.

Consigliere Big Time Dick, as Maureen Dowd[13] named Cheney—he even resembles Robert Duvall—emerged from his hospital bed and took over. How could a man without a heart have a heart attack?[14] He declared Gore a 'sore loser.' Indeed, 'Sore-Loserman' bumper stickers appeared on Republican cars.

Still in a state of shock, Don Preppy told W to just follow Uncle Dick's advice. In an accidental, spontaneous moment with the press, W said: 'Dick Cheney and I will become President and Vice President.' In that order! Don Preppy Georgio shakes his head, sighs. What to do with these slips of the tongue? Hey, Americans have long admired mediocrity in high places. In the great heartland of America he had listened to many politicians talking nonsense to their constituents. Indeed, they used their incoherence as a method to earn their reputations as 'steady.' The Bush family does not chuckle over jokes that imply that W majored in English as a second language.

Poor W wonders how he can survive this messy time without a drink. He needed one badly during the debates. He watches his dad down double martinis to relax before he delivers his own partial-sentence orders to his heir to the secular American throne.

Bush the elder savors, 'payback time,' when his team and family beat the hated rivals who had removed him from the presidency four years before he was ready. He has had to designate W, the oldest progeny, the heir apparent—not because of his intelligence or ability—to become figurehead for the new imperial dynasty. The Bushes will have thousands of jobs to offer loyal retainers, hundreds of billions of dollars to manipulate for those deemed worthy. And, who knows, there's a world out there to win. That, after all, was the grand prize that the Prizzi Bushes sought.

LATER IN JANUARY ...*

The Bushies' legislative agenda will be borrowed from Ronald Reagan: emit heavy conservative rhetoric and make the fanatics happy, but, most importantly, use power to make money for your family and friends and intimidate everyone else.

Given the Senate's 50–50 split they will not quickly repay the National Rifle Association that wants each family to place at least one howitzer in its back yard, but they will try. Nor will they satisfy the most fanatic of Christian soldiers who demand an immediate overturn of *Roe* v. *Wade* and the outlawing of all abortions. But the Bush Prizzis will go through the motions, or at least say the right words about these peripheral matters. Oppose stem cell research, cut affirmative action, funnel taxpayers' money to right-wing religious foundations—but most crucial, cut taxes for the very rich. If an opportunity arises, such as Iraq invading Kuwait as it did in 1990, seize it and become a great president by going to war.

Don Preppy Georgio listens to the pundits and judges babble endlessly about the rule of law. He chuckles. He knows the law of rule. He has played national security games with the law since his CIA days. He remembers how lawyers and spinsters once covered up his involvement in the 1980s Iran-

---

*   Originally appeared as a radio commentary on *Pacifica Network News* and later in the *Anderson Valley Advertiser*, January 3, 2001 (substantially revised for the book).

Contra scandals by pleading that he had amnesia. Now they have covered up some outrageous election thuggery by claiming they were simply following the law, by appearing reasonable. They will be well paid.

Don Preppy hopes that some ambitious media character will not catch W drinking or using drugs—or find one of his old boozing and snorting buddies to go public. He fears that the poor lad will not control those still vivid impulses. He also hopes that the twin granddaughters will not appear as surprise centerfolds in *Playboy*.

For his own future fear—death—he applies the martini remedy. The Boodles bottle enhances that smug pleasure he gets from revenge against the other team, a sentiment that has sweetened his old age. He no longer dallies with a mistress. Barbara smiles a lot, which gives him pleasure. Yes, he thinks, American democracy, what a wonderful system.

CLINTON'S FAREWELL ADDRESS
(Rejected by Some White House Staffer)*

A DREAM!

Bill Clinton, who preceded the beady-eyed W as the beneficiary of the world's most wonderful electoral 'system,' suffered an attack of conscience just before his farewell address—better late than never—and asked me to write his speech.
'But I would write the truth,' I told him.
He sighed. 'Alright, if you must.'

The White House staffers rejected this draft for President Clinton's farewell. So, I share it—complete with instructions to the President—with my readers.

My fellow Americans, George Washington warned us of the dangers of entering into entangling alliances. He also never told a lie (wait for laughter to subside). I wish that I had that strength of character to repress the devil in my soul that induced me to say things like I didn't inhale or have sex with that woman. But a person is who he is. I am what I am (wait for shouts of 'tell 'em Bill!' to abate).

Despite Washington's warning, and especially in the last 60 years, we've certainly entangled ourselves with the world. And I added to that snarl. I mean, I promoted globalization, the process whereby our major corpora-

---

Originally appeared as a radio commentary on *Pacifica Network News* and later in the *Anderson Valley Advertiser*, January 24, 2001 (substantially revised for the book). Written on the eve of Bush's January 20 inauguration.

tions combine with their overseas branches and subsidiaries and receive government subsidies to ease the transition. Some of the Wall Street tycoons and corporate CEOs thanked me personally—and you know how those guys give thanks (wait for nervous laughter to subside). Yes, we raised big bucks during my years in office. GATT, NAFTA, and the WTO have helped realize the fondest dreams of our entrepreneurial class. It has been freed to invest any and everywhere—well, almost—with government tax breaks of course (applause expected).

Eventually, I hope, some of these fine corporate leaders will see their way to allowing labor to organize in those remote countries and will understand that their current environmental practices are incompatible with the future of human life on earth. I'm hopeful that the guys who I invited to sleep in the Lincoln bedroom absorbed some of his conscience (applause).

Traditionally, farewell addresses encourage presidents to voice their special concerns to Congress. In his farewell speech, Dwight Eisenhower warned us of the perils of the growing military–industrial complex. Since then, the military–industrial complex has become institutionalized. I had little choice but to use it when we got into trouble. I had to bomb Iraq, not just to distract attention from my personal problems, but because American presidents cannot tolerate disobedience from the Saddam Husseins of the world (loud applause). I also ordered the bombing of Kosovo to teach that disobedient Slobodan Milosevic a lesson (even louder applause).

But I have accepted, as have my predecessors, Fidel Castro's disobedience, since we learned in Vietnam never to fight an enemy who will fight back. The Pentagon assures me that Cubans will fight back if we go in there to liberate them and estimates a high number of US casualties over a period of years. I confess that I blew the Cuba issue. I should have lifted the embargo and given them a chance to join NAFTA. Well, no one's perfect (audience rises to its feet and applauds). But I did return the little Elian kid to his father. I may have waited longer than I should have, but I did the right thing.

I led the country into eight years of prosperity and peace (more applause from Democrats). I have no apologies on the general achievement, except I did screw up on healthcare. I really wanted a single payer program (expect shouts of yes, yes). But when truly heavy enemies confront me, like the health insurance companies, I back down. I guess my mother taught me to fight only if I could win.

I wish I had the honesty of Washington, the courage of Lincoln, and the grit and innate wisdom of Franklin Roosevelt. Their deeds spoke louder than words (immense applause). Courage in politics, I've discovered, means accepting the limits of power and keeping campaign promises, except of course when I change my mind. I wish I could do it all again.

My agenda for eight years was to govern. And I did that. I let events determine my priorities and I let other issues slide where they slid. I admit that I thought Americans would be ready for new twists on peripheral issues, like letting gays into the military and announcing 'don't ask, don't tell' as a proper approach to one's sexual proclivities. Heck, on reflection, I should have used that as my answer when those reporters kept asking me about my activities (nervous laughter expected).

Maybe another member of my family will preside in the near future and will show that she's learned from my mistakes (applause), but until then we live with what we have. I admit I do sort of like the little fella who's coming next. He'll give you a few laughs, maybe a little heartburn (wait a second for chuckles to fade). Anyway, if anything really important arises, I think you're really gonna miss me (whistles, applause).

WHY BUSH BOMBED BAGHDAD*

Ideology plays a minute part in Washington's imperial thrust. All members of the 'team' assume empire to be axiomatic. Decisions like bombing or even going to war against countries that cannot offer serious resistance often relate more to domestic political concerns than to US geo-strategic interests.

I asked my Washington national security source why Bush bombed Baghdad?

'To show toughness to those Americans and foreigners who thought him both immoral and weak,' he said.

Bush said we bombed to protect the lives of our pilots, I said.

'Don't be gullible,' he replied. 'We've been bombing Iraq for ten years. We've unloaded thousands of tons of explosives on those bad guys from Baghdad to keep freedom alive, stop Iraq from invading her neighbors and from developing weapons of mass destruction and to punish Saddam for violating UN resolutions.'

But, I said, Israel invades her neighbors, has developed weapons of mass destruction and violates more UN resolutions than Iraq.

---

* Originally appeared on *Pacifica Network News* and later in the *Anderson Valley Advertiser*, February 21, 2001 (substantially revised for the book). The White House spinners anticipated that George W. Bush would accomplish little on his first trip abroad to Mexico as president. Coincidentally, he ordered the air force to bomb Baghdad. That made headlines!

'What do you want, consistency?' he retorted. 'Israel has a powerful lobby here and no oil. Hell, our government warned Saddam to keep his planes out of the no-fly zone over his own territory.'

What is the no-fly zone anyway? I asked.

'Nothing to do with the lack of a zipper on your pants, heh heh. America and her junior partner, England, invented the phrase. The US is supposedly protecting some Iraqi minorities that Saddam threatened, although it doesn't really care about them. US and British media repeat this no-fly zone phrase often enough that everyone thinks it's like a UN restriction,' he chuckled.

Why did Bush bomb last week? I asked.

'Well,' he said, 'Clinton bombed Iraq, Sudan and Afghanistan during the worst of the Monica affair. Then during the impeachment episode, he bombed Iraq again.'[15]

I can understand that distraction of public attention, I said, but why would W bomb Baghdad just as he makes his first trip abroad, to Mexico?

'Well, since nothing was gonna happen on that trip, our government thought it would refocus the media. Instead of reporting that W's first foreign trip produced zero, TV would show him as a guy who knows how to hit. Eventually, we'll have to take out Saddam. So keep whacking at him.'

How about those Iraqi kids who've suffered a decade of US punishment? And Saddam hasn't missed a meal.

'Hey,' he quipped, 'like old lady Halfbright [Madeleine Albright], the former secretary of state, said: You can't worry about casualties and at the same time protect the interests of the people who run this country.[16] What are you, some kind of bleeding heart humanitarian? Anyway, not to worry, the media knows that when Israelis get hurt, the press run pictures, but when the ragheads—I mean Iraqis—get bombed, well, they're not real people. Hey, gotta go to a press briefing!'

And then the world changed.

Part II

The Empire Strikes Back

September 11, 2001

9/11 has become a shorthand for feelings and facts, a code for inspiring hatred for others, superficial unity at home; a numerical acronym for fear and repression, violence and war. It also marks a watershed in history.

'Did you see the TV?' my friend asked on the phone at 6 a.m. 'I think a plane hit the New York World Trade Center and exploded. Turn the TV on. It's terrible. I'm scared.'

I watched in disbelief as did tens of millions of others. Then the second plane hit. Soon after, the networks reported that a third plane had struck the Pentagon in Washington. Images appeared on the screen of the destroyed and burning symbol of military power. Yes, it was scary just as my friend said. The fourth hijacked plane apparently had crashed in a field in Pennsylvania killing everyone on board.

My phone rang. I called others. Wow, we all said. Confusion reigned. Tower One collapsed, followed shortly after by its twin. At the time, 'experts' (the bane of our time) estimated as many as 10,000 people might have perished.

How would the weak and intellectually challenged President Bush respond to such an outrage? The media reported that for security reasons he had hidden, first aboard Air Force One and then inside a safe military shelter in the Middle West. When first told of the horrible events, Bush kept smiling and reading to a group of Florida primary students, as if the information hadn't quite sunk in. As Bush and Cheney hibernated and their absence began to look downright weird, the Mayor of New York, Rudolph Giuliani, emerged as a leader, the man in charge and on whose desk the buck stops.

Leaders of the world, from the ass-kissing Tony Blair of England to the disobedience record holder Fidel Castro of Cuba, sent sympathy and offered to help. 'We're all Americans,' read posters in many countries.

I reluctantly turned off the TV. 'A bad time in world history has just begun,' I told my wife before we went to bed.

She agreed. Given the opportunity to show force, the US government would not likely honor contracts and compacts of the past. George W. Bush's planners and speechwriters had already begun to write the document that would shape US relations with the rest of the world and its own citizens. The government would not ask questions about why the attack occurred, what the terrorists might have wanted, or even what ideology or theology had inspired the suicide squad.

Instead, the President labeled these heroic evil-doers 'cowards' and simply stated they 'hate us because we're free.' He announced that the world would launch yet another abstract war that would cost trillions and endure forever.

The war against terrorism, like that against drugs, crime, poverty, cancer and drunk-driving, would define the next decade or more.

FIRST POST-9/11 REFLECTIONS ON GOVERNMENT 'LOGIC'*

The following impressions and analysis of events intend to portray small pieces of the political portrait of our age.

The President said the terrorists had struck America because the nation represented freedom. Then the Attorney General, John Ashcroft, argued for restricting the freedom of US citizens as the way to respond to terrorism. Republican Senator Orrin Hatch of Utah and Democratic Senator Dianne Feinstein from California demanded increased defense funding and immediate retaliation against Osama bin Laden, the Darth Vader of our time. Senior officials of the administration referred to the 9/11 deeds as acts of war, likening them to Pearl Harbor, but no one specified exactly what the enemy wanted.

After all, their behavior points rather toward men with a mission, who plotted with cool and calculating accuracy and then proved themselves more than willing to die for their cause. But what exactly is their cause, other than hating us because we're free? Shouldn't people in power have asked that question and debated it before rushing madly around the world with troops, missiles and extreme belligerence?

Since the assault, Americans have ingested a TV, radio and print diet of bombast, hyperbole and sheer nonsense. The messages from our elected leaders, so-called 'experts' and TV anchors have stressed retaliation and technological security. With box cutters and crude knives, the hijackers commandeered four airplanes; then, determined to commit suicide, the terrorists-cum-pilots steered three planes into symbolic targets of finance and militarism—occupied by real people and leaving real survivors.

Spin doctors tried to convince people that they'd feel better locking the proverbial barn door even though the horses had already escaped. Yet locking doors means losing freedom. Only Democratic Senator Christopher Dodd from Connecticut warned that the terrorists would win if the government responded by restricting civil liberties in the name of security.

The Senate, established by the Founding Fathers to deliberate issues, avoided meaningful discussion and simply granted, as did the House,

---

*   Appeared in *Anderson Valley Advertiser*, September 19, 2001. Originally published as 'The questions not asked as the Empire strikes back' and substantially revised for the book.

billions of dollars to the President to use as he wished. Congress will pour money into military and police operations, under the curious rubric of security—a far cry from a thumb and a blanket—while destroying the fiscal soundness of social security, education, Medicare and environmental protection plans. The elected officials responded in panic to White House threats and empty rhetoric. 'The terrorist threat demands money,' asserts the President. 'Hand it over!'

Congress replies, 'Yes, sir.'

Real security based on traditional rights and a concern for the common welfare has become transformed into the new security. In fact, the omnipresent 'security' officials produce the opposite—anxiety.

Over the years, 'national security' has euphemistically blanketed a series of crimes, like overthrowing governments and starting foolish wars. Between 1970 and 1973, US officials conspired to overthrow the socialist government of Chile. Over five plus decades the United States has backed Israel almost unconditionally in wars against its neighbors and the Palestinians. The government declared as 'national security' threats the national liberation movements in Vietnam, Laos and Cambodia. Indeed, five consecutive presidents, from Eisenhower to Ford, 1958–1975, ordered the bombing and napalming of those people and lands. Reagan and Bush (41) carried out terrorist campaigns against Nicaragua from 1980 to 1989, and backed ruling military murderers in El Salvador and Guatemala. US planes have regularly bombed Iraq and they have carried out 'missions' in Yugoslavia, Sudan and Afghanistan. For 43 years, the US government has sponsored formally and informally terrorist campaigns and assassination plans against Cuba. Presidents have used the 'needs' of 'national security,' to justify all these activities, some acknowledged, some denied, but all documented.

Now, bin Laden and his cult have successfully stepped into a world that everyone believed belonged mainly to the CIA plotters. The Bush White House responded both emotionally and opportunistically, threatening to bomb those Taliban brutes who harbor bin Laden in Afghanistan back into the Stone Age. How do you successfully threaten with death those who welcome it? It matters not to those who make the bombs or earn their living through military violence.

Do the September 11 events dramatize a real clash of civilizations? Do the attacks on the real and symbolic nerve centers of world finance and militarism mean real war against corporate globalization—a war that most of us anti-globalization types want no part of?

The world witnessed in 1979 Iran and in post-communist Afghanistan some signs of what the purifiers of Islam want. It's not what I had in mind when I opposed corporate globalization. I don't want my daughters to grow up uneducated, with covered faces and trailing their husbands; nor do I want a theocracy dedicated to setting the world back five centuries.

However, I do not want to go to war with innocent people in the name of responding to the September 11 stone cold killers. I think the time has come to study, think, and debate. Then, when the public has been informed and not confused by national security managers and confused by a driven media, the US government should act, in concert with the rest of the civilized world, with police ruthlessness and legality.

THE TRIVIALIZED LOGIC OF OUR TIME*

Almost like a Rilke poem, political logic flows: words upon words upon words, followed by images upon images upon images—but without poetry.

After September 11, US officials offered yet another strange brand of logic to the apparently accepting American public. Although the terrorists appeared to have had their headquarters, funding and religious roots in Saudi Arabia, the US government somehow destroyed their infrastructure by bombing Afghanistan, the place where their key banker, bin Laden, temporarily resided and had some temporary training camps. Indeed, reliable public sources show that Saudi Arabia even financed the Taliban regime in Afghanistan and provided it with military support there as well.

So, the Bush government proceeds to obliterate Afghanistan, even though Al-Qaeda, the shadowy terrorist organization involved in the 9/11 attacks, has hundreds of cells throughout the world. The logic apparently relies on the assumption that the US can destroy all of Al-Qaeda by finding and eliminating bin Laden, thought still to be hiding in Afghanistan. Thousands of bombs dropped on his suspected lairs and thousands of US troops sent to hunt him down have failed to find him.

According to one wit, bin Laden has proven as elusive as the Vice President, Dick Cheney, code named Waldo, the obscure figure hiding on the cover of puzzle boxes. Parker Brothers may even develop a new board game, called 'Find Dick and Osama.'

---

* First appeared on *Pacifica Network News* and *Anderson Valley Advertiser*, and later in *Progreso Weekly* (www.rprogreso.com), November 22, 2001. Written a little over a month after the commencement of the US-led coalition bombing of Afghanistan. *Progreso Weekly* is a Miami-based weekly online magazine in English and Spanish offering coverage of South Florida politics and world news.

Despite the apparent holes in the White House argument, the President has sold Congress on still another piece of his post-9/11 logic. To improve the inadequate work of the FBI and CIA, the citizens must now cede their liberties. This surrender of basic rights will magically transform the dreary performances of these agencies pre-9/11 into stellar examples of police and intelligence operations in the post-9/11 period.

Under the new anti civil liberties rules, the FBI has already shown its power in quantitative terms: within a month, it detained some 1,200 people in connection with the September 11 horrors.[17] Apparently, as subsequent investigations showed, few of those arrested had even the remotest links with the grizzly 9/11 events. But the FBI insisted that it had to deny their basic rights in order to prove its own competence. You figure!

Trust the FBI, pleaded the Attorney General, John Ashcroft. They know what they're doing. Sure! Take their investigation of the anthrax case. The anthrax ghoul mailed his toxin to leading members of the Senate and selected mass media representatives. But several postal workers and others picked up the germ presumably during routine mail handling. The super-sleuths, at least as Americans see them portrayed on TV and in the movies, found almost no leads. The FBI had to appeal to the public for help in finding the source of the anthrax mailings. They didn't even have a picture to put on the TV show *America's Most Wanted*.

Ashcroft himself, however, has become a unique TV personality. He repeatedly warns the public of yet another imminent terrorist attack. He never gives details about where and when, or of the nature of the impending attack because that's 'classified,' known only to law enforcement officials and the terrorists. These announcements supposedly induce the public to remain calm and prepared for new assaults.

A Washington source told me that the intelligence heavies' biggest fear involves some 'missing' Stinger missiles, the kind fired from a shoulder at an airplane. The CIA delivered more than 500 of these weapons to the mujaheddin in Pakistan in the 1980s, but after they defeated the Soviet-backed regime in 1992, the United States' loyal clients didn't return the hundreds of unused weapons.[18]

In light of such facts, some wise and worried counselors have repeated to Bush the late Vermont senator George Aiken's advice to Lyndon Johnson on Vietnam strategy back in 1966: 'Declare victory and come home!'[19] Bush could say: 'We've destroyed their training camps. Thanks to the bombing of Afghanistan we haven't had a serious terrorist attack in two months, and I'm bringing the troops home.' Unfortunately, much of the counsel he's hearing comes from ambitious fools and relates to expanding the war to Iraq—a kind of bureaucratic 'creeping mission syndrome' that occurs when military campaigns don't achieve their ends.

Bush should study—too strong a word?—Johnson's and Richard Nixon's experiences. LBJ responded to military failure in Vietnam by sending more troops into battle. US casualties multiplied. Nixon, learning from Johnson's mistake, withdrew US troops and increased aerial bombing. He also foolishly expanded the war to Cambodia and paid a political price. So, Bush, not one for studying, seems to walk unwittingly along the path of old and twisted illogic, one that has resulted not only in military and political failure but in a debilitating 'syndrome' that has affected several generations.

Sadly, the major media does not use its critical facilities—its eyes or lenses—to penetrate this 'logic.' It continues to believe the patent nonsense of government officials. The comedian Richard Pryor understood the paradox.

His wife discovers him in bed with a naked woman.

'Hey, sugar, it's not what you think,' says Pryor.

'What? Are you crazy? I'm seeing this with my own eyes,' she says.

'Hey, honey,' says Pryor, 'who ya gonna believe, me or your lying eyes?'

Ashcroft has indeed become a collector of names and facts about the people who live in the United States. He has also developed what scientists call a helix. In government this translates as:

FAILURE EQUALS BIGGER BUDGET, MORE POWER: The Domestic Shift of Empire*

The Attorney General, Ashcroft, and Robert Mueller III, the Director of the FBI, implicitly blamed the FBI's failure to stop the 9/11 attacks on the citizens. Yes, because Americans possessed so much freedom, the FBI felt disadvantaged.

So, Ashcroft has taken steps to rectify this imbalance between rights and performance: Citizens, cede your civil liberties and constitutional rights and the FBI will protect you from the next terrorist attack. Even easier, Congress will cede them for you.

Few members of Congress challenged the Attorney General's unspoken assertion. If they had, they might have discovered that the 'logic' of Ashcroft and Mueller doesn't exactly correspond with the facts. In reality, the

---

* Originally appeared in *Progreso Weekly*, June 13, 2002. Each week bits of news oozed from the media about the CIA and FBI's failures to prevent the 9/11 attacks and these agencies' need for larger budgets.

enjoyment by US citizens of their rights and liberties played no part in impeding the Bureau from discovering Al-Qaeda plots.

Worse, after 9/11, FBI big shots demoted Colleen Rowley, a supervisor of the Minneapolis office, for writing a clear and cogent memo to her boss following the attacks. Rowley stated that national security issues should prevail over the Bureau's traditional huffy response to criticism.[20] But Mueller and his cronies still use J. Edgar Hoover's tried and true formula: outraged denial as a means to cover your ass. Hey, what should a woman agent expect when she criticizes a Bureau directed by 100 per cent macho men? Well, sort of, if you recall Hoover's alleged passion for wearing tutus in his living room!

Rather than communicate with each other about truly serious issues, the apparatchiks in both agencies remained stuck in their decades-old bureaucratic turf wars. What's a top government post about anyway if not the size of one's budget?

If Ashcroft had real dignity, he would have quit after firing his immediate underlings for proving inadequate in the face of the nation's most serious security issue. Instead, he tacitly charged the First Amendment with preventing the Bureau from doing its job. At a December 6, 2001 hearing before the Senate Judiciary Committee, Ashcroft claimed that security demanded that liberties take a back seat to security. 'To those who scare peace-loving people with phantoms of lost liberty, my message is this,' he said. 'Your tactics only aid terrorists, for they erode our national unity and diminish our resolve. They give ammunition to America's enemies ...' Yes, Ashcroft wants us to believe that we never had the liberties we just lost and that the FBI failed to protect the nation because we were enjoying too much constitutional freedom.

On February 1, 2001, the cowardly Democrats in Congress confirmed as Attorney General this inept, ultra right-winger who lost in his re-election bid for the Senate from Missouri to a dead man.[21] Ashcroft's grim demeanor reminds me of H.L. Mencken's definition of Puritanism: 'the haunting fear that someone, somewhere, may be happy.'[22]

I wonder whether Ashcroft really wants to get Al-Qaeda or if he just hates freedom in almost any form that might yield pleasure and happiness—like looking at a well-crafted statue in one's work place, even if the statue portrays the bare human form. According to news reports, last year Ashcroft, in his Protestant version of Taliban behavior, spent more than $8,000 of taxpayer money to place a *burkha* over the bare breast of a statue that has long stood in the Department of Justice.[23]

In the 1960s and 1970s Congress failed to exercise control of the FBI during its attempts to simulate the Gestapo. Before approving any of Ashcroft's 'new' requests Congress should recall how the FBI under Hoover battered civil liberties until they were barely recognizable. Under the guise of identifying foreign agents, the Bureau set out to disrupt the anti-war and civil rights movements by placing agents provocateurs inside virtually every organization. In 1972, former FBI special agent Robert Wall described how some agents turned 'informants' into provocateurs and lawbreakers. Wall said he resigned from the Bureau in the early 1970s because 'my job seemed to consist of countless hours spying on citizens exercising their basic rights, people who had committed no crime.'[24]

In 1972, I produced a segment for *The Great American Dream Machine* (aired on WNET) in which one 'informant' said on camera that in 1970 his FBI special agent had ordered him to burn down a University of Alabama dormitory so that radicals would be blamed; another said on camera that he had been ordered to bomb a Seattle post office. The FBI had snatched these 'informants' from local police who had arrested them on drug charges. Bureau 'excesses' of this kind became public when an unknown party broke into FBI offices at Media, Pennsylvania in 1977 and stole Bureau files that documented these and other instances of illegal FBI activity.

The FBI recruited many of its 'informants' from a pool of losers. The Bureau agents would enter city jails, confront a 'perp' in his cell and often threaten him with harsh prison terms; or, on the other hand, offer to drop charges if he would work for the FBI.

Because of these well-documented abusive practices, the FBI agreed in 1975 to accept a set of guidelines that would allow them to do their jobs without abusing State police power. Then came 9/11.

Now, Ashcroft and his deputy Mueller simply inform us that they must scrap these guidelines in order to prevent future terrorist acts. Without consulting Congress or the courts, Ashcroft authorized FBI agents to investigate individuals and groups for up to one year on 'suspicion.' They no longer need in *New York Times* columnist William Safire's words 'a scintilla of evidence that a crime is being committed.'[25]

Behind all of this 'conservative' patter and emergency rhetoric, Ashcroft adheres to the trusted Washington adage: nothing succeeds like failure. The bigger the screw up—like not stopping the 9/11 attackers—the more you're entitled to. Remember, of course, to label the demand for a bigger budget by some euphemism like 'reorganization for the new security threat.'

Congress, pay attention! Ashcroft needs a new math equation. How about: the real agents of the terrorists equal those who seek to erode our freedoms in the name of efficiently combating terrorism!

THE BIRTH OF THE DEPARTMENT
OF PERPETUAL ANXIETY*

Gore Vidal, the great novelist and political critic, asked me how I liked living under the dictatorship. I laughed, but I felt a chill. Americans have now experienced nine months of life under unusual circumstances and it's time for reflection about the state of their democracy. We have moved quickly from life inside a tenuous republic that jostled with a national security state into an overtly imperial mode.

President George W. Bush must have just seen a re-run of John Huston's 1948 film The Treasure of the Sierra Madre *and paraphrased to Congress what the Mexican bandit told Humphrey Bogart. In the movie, the bandit chief unconvincingly pretends he is a policeman and when Bogey asks him to show his badge as proof, the bandit responds: 'I don't got to show you no stinkin' badge.'*

Now, Congress pleads with Bush to show them reasons for his decision to expand the 'war on terrorism' beyond Afghanistan to Yemen, the Caucasus, Colombia, the Philippines, Iraq and wherever else his advisers suggest. Improving on the performance of the screen bandit, he tells Congress: 'I don't got to show you no stinkin' reasons.' Unlike the bad guy, Bush, the presidential thief, has some real support—Congress itself!

In his 2000 election campaign, the conservative George W. promised a smaller government, so that democracy could work better. Traditionally, 'small government' has meant that the propertied interests could exercise control over state and local governments with less money and effort than it would take to dominate the national machinery. But the innate laws of bureaucracy exercise their own power.

When the White House proposed the creation of a new Ministry of Homeland Security, I asked myself: Why do Americans need yet another security agency? There exists just on the federal level, the CIA, the DIA, the NSA, the FBI, the INS, the AFT, the DEA, and God knows how many other police agencies, alongside the panoply of defense and nuclear security agencies. Have the Bushies redefined Republican principles by converting the once evil idea of big government into a biblical essential?

How did the United States survive without this new agency to protect the American homeland, secure our borders, transportation, ports and critical infrastructure, by synthesizing and analyzing homeland security intelligence from multiple sources and coordinating efforts to protect the American people against bio-terrorism and other weapons of mass destruction? No one mentioned such an idea after the 1995 Oklahoma City bombing, the terrorist revenge act carried out by a red-blooded, white American man, with

---

* Originally appeared in *Progreso Weekly*, July 22, 2002. Written after the White House announced the creation of another department.

a distinguished military background. Only when some mysterious Muslims struck did the pious right-wingers abandon Reagan's old saw about trusting the private sector and demand more government power.

In his campaign, Bush swore to shrink government. Now he can't enlarge it enough. Has he become a convert to Franklin Roosevelt's New Deal, where government agencies proliferated like mushrooms in shit? Come to think of it, the New Deal agencies tried to bring economic recovery not destroy the economy.

How will the government fund the Department of Homeland Security when it can't raise taxes? W's daddy went back on his word and had to raise them, resulting—some Republicans believe—in his 1992 election defeat. He had forgotten what he had learned at the knee of the modern Republican icon.

Ronald Reagan established the political lesson for the 1980s: love your private sector—'bidness'—and hate your government. The public apparently liked Reagan so much that even the Democrats began to sing this atonal hymn. Indeed, Clinton solved some of the nastier Republican problems, ones that Reagan wouldn't dirty his hands with—like abolishing welfare and balancing the budget.

Reagan re-established the words 'Republican Party' to apply to the conservative. Reckless or foolish better describes it. But his rhetoric and popularity forced even the middle-of-the-road Democrats to abandon their 'profligate' spending habits on social issues. Reagan told the country that he cut taxes because it was the right thing to do and that not only his contributors, friends and relatives but everyone would somehow benefit. He had that reassuring smile when he explained such incongruous notions and the folks believed him.

But Reagan's vision had severe limits. In contrast, in less than two years, W had extended the Empire to places that even the most hawkish expansionists never dreamed of, places Bush himself couldn't have identified even by continent—like Georgia, which he thought was part of the United States until Condy Rice gave him a few geography lessons. (She forgot to mention, however, before Bush met with Brazilian President Henrique Cardoso that Brazil had more blacks than the United States. When the Brazilian President visited the White House on March 30, 2001, Bush purportedly asked Cardoso if Brazil had any blacks.[26])

'Live and learn,' the President said. Well, maybe just live! But he sounds so assured, so certain, when he talks.

But Bush's audience doesn't include Congress. Indeed, he refuses to share the little information he has with legislators, citing 'national security' reasons, of course. He also instructed Homeland Security chief, Tom Ridge, to refuse to divulge information to the body that used to make the laws. Indeed, Ridge finally and reluctantly made his appearance before Congress in the late spring 2002, but revealed little. Did he have anything to reveal?

So what's going on? Do Americans need a new ministry to deal with the periodic warnings of another terrorist attack? Do they need yet another high official who offers them no details about where and when or how to prepare? Have the Bushies turned into the little boy who cried wolf on one hand and nuclear bullies threatening pre-emptive bombing strikes on the other?

Look at their accomplishments at home. On June 10, 2002 Ashcroft announced that the government had arrested on May 8—note the month plus discrepancy—a former Chicago gang member and charged him with plotting as an Al-Qaeda agent to explode a dirty (nuclear tipped) bomb.[27] By naming Jose Padilla an 'enemy combatant'[28] the Department of Justice circumvented all constitutional procedures. Padilla, a US citizen, lost his right to an attorney, habeas corpus and to hear charges against him. Just as skeptics raised questions about a new government agency, the President's advisers and followers gloated.

'See,' they insisted, 'we told you it was a dangerous world.'

And now, with Padilla locked up without rights, Americans are safer?

Even former CIA chief and defense secretary James Schlesinger (of the Nixon and Ford days) asked how the US government manufactured an immediate Al-Qaeda threat out of an uneducated US citizen who had no access to radioactive material and did not know how to make a bomb. A June 11 *New York Times* editorial accused Ashcroft of exaggerating 'the likely damage when he said such a bomb could cause "mass death and injury".' But the Ashcroft-spun headline said: 'US says it halted Al-Qaeda plot to use radioactive bomb.' Does it not drive up one's anxiety level?

After Bush assumed the presidential office in January 2001, a friend of mine suggested we might as well just enjoy life under a mediocre president. Bush might follow the predictable and relatively uneventful course of Calvin Coolidge in the 1920s. Instead, an imperial monster has emerged, an expansionist whose vision (albeit muddled) outstrips those of the presidents—all Democrats, by the way—who launched the nation into the great twentieth-century wars: from Woodrow Wilson (World War I), FDR (World War II), and Truman (Korea) to Kennedy and Johnson (Vietnam). The so-called 1991 Gulf War, on reflection, appears more of a technological massacre than a war, given that the enemy didn't fight back.

This previously underachieving man has revealed an imposing leitmotif. By declaring war against terrorism he has engaged with both a formless and presumably chronic foe.

The Republican Party, no longer conservative by any definition that Edmund Burke could have accepted, redefines itself a day at a time; not a bad situation for a supposedly recovering alcoholic president.

The Bushies now take the offensive by embracing the born-again logic of 'don't let anyone get to the right of you on military and security policies.' Under the label of urgent patriotism they cover up mistakes and make a new agency for their own re-election security.

ELECTION SORROWS AND COLD ANALYSIS:
Democrats Blew It Again but US Elections Have Little to Do with Democracy*

Indeed, the war against terrorism did emit vibrations that resulted in political paralysis, especially for the Democrats, who never learned how to present themselves as an opposition force on foreign and defense issues. The terrorism theme also reverberated among the electorate. Do the urge for protection against unknown terrorists and the need to shop reduce the importance of voting?

Before I allowed my gloom over the results of the November 5, 2002 elections to become permanent, I confronted some facts and statistics. About 38 per cent of eligible American voters cast ballots, hardly a majority; not a mandate for war or cutting taxes.

Indeed, the vote represented anything but a go-ahead sign for W. The margin between victory and defeat for control of the Congress came down to 29,000 votes in Minnesota, 11,500 in Missouri and 9,500 in New Hampshire.[29] Had Democrats actually voted, their Party would have controlled the upper house and the pundits would have reported about how Bush's hitting the campaign trail proved to be a fatal error. Give credit to Svengali Karl Rove, Bush's adviser and chief architect of Republican strategy who once again outwitted the Democratic National Committee (DNC) Chair, Terry 'Boris Badinoff' McAuliffe.

The Democrats appear to have done all in their power to keep their own voters at home while Republicans, as usual, turned out their flocks. Rich Republicans always understand that by electing their candidates, they will pay lower taxes and have fewer problems with the hired help. By the mid 1960s, Republican strategists had understood that they couldn't win any more national elections if they remained just the party of the rich. So, from

---

* Originally appeared in *Progreso Weekly*, November 14, 2002. On November 5, 2002, the US held congressional, state and local elections.

1964 on when Barry Goldwater of Arizona won the nomination for president, the Republican Party also began to actively represent fanatics as well as millionaires.

The Republican army of God obediently turned out to vote for the special interests of the rich and the zealots. Instead of following their class interests, these poor robots formed an alliance around peripheral issues: anti-abortion, pro-gun rights and prayer in school as the answer to the moral unease of our times.

Maybe Democrats didn't vote because they don't have a real political party. My parents, New Deal Democrats, appreciated that Franklin Roosevelt stood for the interests of the poor and the needy. Sure, he compromised with reactionary segregationists. But the party nonetheless sent a message that working people, most Catholics, blacks, Jews, and other minorities understood. The modern Democratic Party, however, represents little more than a modern money-laundering machine.

One friend questioned my premise and talked about tradition and how some people still vote Republican because their grandpas did. Maybe, but I don't think that African Americans or solid Midwestern conservatives voted Republican because Lincoln freed the slaves or Eisenhower won World War II—well, sort of. Blacks just didn't vote in the number needed for Democratic victories.

In the South, traditionally staunch Democrats yawned over the non-messages flowing from the mouths of their party's candidates. 13,000 fewer voters than four years ago turned out in the Georgia County with the largest number of black voters. Unlike black voters, Latinos actually found some attractive qualities in Republican candidates, especially those who learned or already knew some Spanish. The Republican National Committee reported that more than 33 per cent of Latino voters went for the Governor of Texas Rick Perry, a man who epitomized the worst of corporate values. Jeb Bush, the Governor of Florida, won re-election with more than 60 per cent of the Latino vote. The Governor of New York, George E. Pataki, got his second term with almost half of the Hispanic vote.[30]

As the issues screamed at the Democrats for attention, they turned deaf. W proposed a tax cut that would make the filthy rich even richer; simultaneously, the cut would diminish the national treasury and make difficult if not impossible funding of basic social programs, like real help to the senior citizens on prescription drug costs. Yes, a few liberal candidates mentioned this issue, but the Democrats as a whole didn't take out major ads and TV spots; nor did national Democratic spokespeople take this issue door to door or talk to people at bus stops or senior citizen centers. So, traditional Democratic voters responded to this energy-less, message-free campaign by shrugging their shoulders and abstaining from the one activity that allows people a smidgen of participation in the political process.

Similarly, the Democrats dropped the ball on corporate scandals, some of which linked directly to Bush and Cheney. Showing Bush's ties to Enron, the energy trading multinational corporation, would have put the Republicans on the defensive. Most important, the pusillanimous Senate Majority leader, Tom Daschle, and the poor excuse for a strategist in the House, Minority leader Dick Gephardt, pushed their colleagues to endorse the lame-brained scheme for expanded and unconstitutional war powers. When Bush, Cheney and Rumsfeld demanded unqualified backing for war against Iraq without offering a fact to support their allegations, the Democrats rallied around the flag.

Those few Democrats who refused to kowtow to cowardice, according to the pollsters, improved their ratings. Indeed, polls show that the majority of Americans oppose unilateral action. But apparently fearful of being branded wimpy, wussy and downright unpatriotic, the Democratic leaders buckled.

What a terrible way to think about politics and publics! Instead of saying, 'I have stated my position and you can vote for me because you agree with me or because you appreciate my integrity,' the Democrats relied on opinion polls to determine their positions. Ironically, those who followed the supposed poll numbers and not a set of principles lost.

The Democrats also refused to take the economic offensive against Bush's scheme to benefit the plutocracy. Instead of slamming his tax cut for the rich, Daschle wavered and, on talk shows, sounded like a namby-pamby. In the *New York Times*, November 9, 2002, Frank Rich quoted Daschle whining to *CNN*'s Paula Zahn: 'We felt we did have the economic plan. We just weren't successful in getting you to cover it.'

What? With lay-offs and rising unemployment, Bush rewards the richest 1 per cent of the country and the Democrats have nothing to say that will make the media respond? With shrinking healthcare coverage—over 70 million have no health insurance[31]—all they can think of is prescription drugs for the elderly? With dramatic corporate scandals involving the theft of billions of dollars from the public, all they can devise is a moderate accounting reform? What did the Democratic candidates stand for? Well, just half-heartedly governing the country—sort of—you know! That means they continue to trade favors for money.

Democratic leaders feared that concrete legislation to help the poor and middle classes might disaffect large corporate givers and hurt the party treasury. The Democrats claimed they represented the little guy but in office helped the big guy. The party remains an olio of corporate executives and union leaders, polluters and environmentalists, landlords and tenants, hawks and doves united by a common blood link to the coffers of the party treasury.

No wonder the Democratic voters had trouble understanding their party's program! The Bushies screamed bomb Saddam, and don't trust the weak and 'tax and spend' liberals. The gun and God lobbies and the paid mouthpieces for the wealthy moguls mobilized their voters.

Now that those minorities have real power, Bush will submit a spate of judicial appointments slightly to the left of Adolf Hitler. Perhaps medical science will perfect the spinal transplant and a few Democrats will filibuster against the appointments of the ultra fanatics who now run the US government in every branch.

The Bushies crafted a clear message, albeit a bogus one: to support the President's tough line on Iraq will make us 'secure.' The majority of Democrats, instead of mocking Bush's unsubstantiated allegations and calling for calm and reason, agreed with W's zany premise and only argued about the means to accomplish it.

Reality will confront voters and non-voters. Unemployment and insecurity over jobs will grow more acute. People will worry more and rightly so about their once-secure retirement plans and dwindling health coverage—for those that have any. If the Democrats don't zoom in on the issues and make daily references to corporate scandals and the phony excuses for war, they will continue to tread water or worse.

Talk like Franklin Roosevelt, I say. He sure got the voters out.

By the way, $1,238,358,891 was spent on the 2002 Democratic campaign in which senators and governors won no more than 10 per cent of the eligible vote.[32]

BUSH APPOINTS KISSINGER TO HEAD WARREN COMMISSION ON 9/11—Instead of Investigating Him for Terrorism*

If the elections led some toward cynicism, imagine the impact on morale when Bush nominated Henry Kissinger to lead an investigation into the breakdowns in the pre-9/11 government bureaucracy.

Bush got the loudest laugh when he appointed the 79-year-old Henry Kissinger to head the investigation into the actions—or inactions—of government agencies around the 9/11 events.

---

*   Appeared in *Progreso Weekly and CounterPunch* (www.counterpunch.org), December 5, 2002. On November 27, 2002, Bush named Henry Kissinger to lead a panel investigating the 9/11 events. The electronic edition of *CounterPunch*, a muckraking newsletter, is edited by Alexander Cockburn and Jeffrey St. Clair from Petrolia, California.

'Ha,' I guffawed, 'the man least likely to reveal the truth, the man least interested in honesty and disclosure, the man with a world-class reputation for spreading and supporting terror in several continents now reigns as commish of a panel to investigate terrorism! Wow! Talk about irony!'

Instead of doing the right thing, investigating Kissinger for his own terrorist acts, Dubya named the sly old fox to investigate mass murder in the proverbial hen house. The public will certainly feel assured—that is, those without memory or the ability to read history.

When Kissinger won the 1973 Nobel Peace Prize after overseeing the slaughter of tens of thousands of Vietnamese civilians in his infamous 1972 Christmas bombing of Hanoi, a friend suggested he should have won the prize for physics.

'What did he know about physics?' I asked, like a straight man.

'Ah ha!' sneered my friend.

Some relatives of the 9/11 victims didn't get the joke when they heard of Bush's decision to dub Henry the chief prober. Why, some asked, appoint a man who had proven his hatred for democracy and much of humanity? But, most of all, why nominate a man who despises truth, especially in its published form?

In the 1970s, the Washington media, living in a world of liars, informally dubbed Henry as an unequaled prevaricator. An apocryphal story from those days has a confounded Washington press corps hiring a shrink and giving him press credentials to observe Kissinger during his infamous media 'background briefings' and provide clues as to when the architect of US foreign policy is lying. After several sessions the shrink tells the reporters: 'It's simple. When Kissinger folds his hands like a German school boy or fiddles with his glasses, he's telling the truth. When he opens his mouth to speak, he's lying.'[33]

W's advisers surely knew that Kissinger stands for governmental honesty as Al Capone symbolizes civic virtue. So the Bushies may well have a non-humorous motive for appointing this mountebank among charlatans.

Remember, W had initially opposed any investigation into 9/11. But after the media revealed that US agencies had foreknowledge of the horrid events, the families of the victims exerted heavy pressure on Bush to go deeper. So, he had to investigate, but didn't want truth to emerge, that is, actual facts to appear in print. It is rare that a government benefits from having the truth revealed and Henry had proved himself as a pro at concealing.

When Kissinger wasn't actually carrying out campaigns of terror and murder in the early and mid 1970s, he spent much of his time lying and covering up his dirty deeds. Back in 1968, Republican Party heavies chose Kissinger to fly to Paris to help sabotage President Johnson's peace talks with the Vietnamese. In his campaign, Nixon had promised to 'end the war with honor.' Kissinger secretly assured the North Vietnam government that if they could hold out and not cut a deal with the Johnson administration, Nixon would make a better peace with them. Nixon rewarded Kissinger for his nefarious behavior by naming him national security adviser. Kissinger rewarded the Vietnamese by prolonging the war, although he knew the United States could not win it. His 'peace with honor' nonsense cost more than a million Vietnamese lives; scores of thousands of US soldiers dead and wounded.

In 1970, Kissinger had helped persuade Nixon to widen the war to include Cambodia. Without congressional authorization or even knowledge, Kissinger presided over the secret bombing and invasion of Cambodia, in an attempt to 'cut off the Ho Chi Minh trail' and deprive the Vietnamese enemy of supplies. No one has yet accurately calculated how many hundreds of thousands of civilians died in this futile terrorist operation. Kissinger and Nixon secretly carried out an aerial war against Cambodia without telling even the joint chiefs of staff. Indeed, the pilots of the bomber planes kept false logs indicating that the Cambodia missions were flown over North Vietnam so as to deceive the joint chiefs and everyone else.

Also in 1970, Kissinger conspired to alter the destiny of Chile. In September 1970, Dr. Salvador Allende, a socialist, won the election to head a popular unity government. With Nixon's approval, Kissinger directed a CIA covert operation to 'destabilize' the government. In October 1970, with Kissinger's knowledge and approval, the CIA tried to assassinate Allende and did assassinate with the help of hired fascist thugs from Patria y Libertad the Chilean army chief, General Rene Schneider, who stood as an obstacle to removing Allende (currently, poor Henry is facing possible legal problems in connection with that murder). The Schneider family has sued K for wrongful death, claiming that documents prove 'that [Kissinger] was involved in great detail in supporting the people who killed General Schneider, and then paid them off.'[34]

In another Chile-related case, Kissinger was asked by Chile's Supreme Court to answer official questions about the murder of an American reporter in Chile shortly after the September 1973 coup. It appears that very high officials in the State Department refused to help Charles Horman (see Constantin Costa Gavras' 1982 film, *Missing*) when Pinochet's Gestapo was torturing and then murdering him.

K denied involvement in the coup from day one, although he chastised the Chilean people for being irresponsible in electing Allende as President. In April 1972, Kissinger arranged to meet Orlando Letelier, Chile's Ambassador to Washington, at a dinner party. 'With no trace of a smile,'

Letelier recounted to me, 'Kissinger wanted me to assure Allende that the US government was not destabilizing the Chilean government.'

Letelier laughed. He knew what was going on in Chile even if Kissinger was covering up his approval of CIA plans to commit violent acts to disrupt Chilean society. When the press corps pushed Kissinger as to why an elected socialist government threatened US security, Kissinger jokingly retorted in 1972: 'Chile is like a dagger pointed at the heart of Antarctica.'[35]

The Chilean military, with CIA urging, finally launched the coup that overthrew the elected government. In its place, a pro-US military junta led by General Augusto Pinochet carried out a long reign of terror, murdering, torturing and exiling its political opponents.

After the coup, Kissinger ordered immediate recognition and aid for the illegal government. In June 1976, he graced Pinochet with a personal visit while most of the world was condemning him for gross violations of human rights. Before delivering a speech at an Organization of American States (OAS) meeting in Chile, K met privately with Pinochet and assured the mass murderer that his forthcoming speech on human rights was not 'directed against your government.'

A State Department transcribed memo of the conversation shows that Kissinger flattered the man whom he knew had murdered thousands including his 'enemies' abroad. 'We are sympathetic to what you are trying to do here,' Kissinger told the tyrant.[36]

Pinochet twice suggested that Letelier was responsible for his bad 'image' throughout the world. Kissinger blamed the 'international left.' He assured Pinochet that Washington supported his methods. I think he meant economic methods and the means he used for establishing 'order.' I don't think K meant to give Pinochet the green light to assassinate Letelier.

But on September 21, 1976, three months later, Pinochet sent his assassins to Washington to car bomb Letelier. Ronni Moffitt, a US colleague at the Institute for Policy Studies where they both worked, also died in the terrorist attack. The FBI discovered that the Letelier car bombing was the work of Operation Condor, a network of Latin American intelligence agencies head-quartered in Chile that carried out surveillance on each other's dissidents and sometimes 'disappeared' and assassinated them in each other's countries. Pinochet had extended his murderous reach beyond the friendly military dictatorships of South America, however. The FBI also discovered that he had set up assassination plots in Rome, London, Paris and Madrid as well. Kissinger knew all about Pinochet's 'methods' before he gave him his Good Housekeeping Seal of Approval.

K, like the Stanley Kubrick film character Dr. Strangelove, possesses an eccentric sense of humor. After having initially backed a Kurdish uprising against Iraq, when Saddam Hussein was only informally running the government during the mid 1970s, he abruptly pulled the rug from under the rebelling Kurds. When a subordinate responded in shock to K's lightning desertion of an ally since he had heard the Secretary promise the Kurds undying loyalty and aid, K quoted the old adage: 'Promise them anything, give them what they get and f... them if they can't take a joke.'[37]

In recent years, however, Kissinger himself has become the butt of a few jokes. In 2001, a Chilean judge investigating Condor has tried to include Kissinger in his witness list. Baltazar Garzon, the Spanish judge who requested the English government to arrest Pinochet in 1998, also wants to question Kissinger about his knowledge of Pinochet's crimes. A French judge presiding over a case involving the kidnapping of French citizens in Chile wants Kissinger to answer questions. Last May, he sent police to a Paris hotel, where Kissinger was staying, to serve him questions. In February, Kissinger canceled a trip to Brazil when he heard that human rights groups would picket him.

In another of his pro-terrorism performances, in December 1975, the jocular Kissinger traveled with President Gerald Ford to Indonesia and tacitly accepted Suharto's request for 'understanding if we deem it necessary to take rapid or drastic action' in East Timor. Ford responded to Suharto after consulting with Kissinger: 'We will understand and will not press you on the issue. We understand the problem you have and the intentions you have.'[38] Suharto's intentions in East Timor were to quickly have the Indonesian armed forces massacre tens of thousands of civilians. Kissinger denied knowledge of this atrocity and lied about it in his memoirs.

K admitted that he preferred dealing with 'authoritarian' regimes (dictatorships) because he found them less troublesome than democracies. So, in 1976 the Argentine foreign minister representing the military dictatorship there described Kissinger as 'euphoric' over their plans for repression. Kissinger's advice was to make the killing quick. This was early in what came to be known as the 'dirty war,' in which with US backing as many as 30,000 died at the hands of the military government.

The man who once loved terrorists as long as they occupied state power and behaved obediently to him is now charged with investigating terrorism used against the master state itself. Even more amazing than K's appointment is the fact that the Democrats accepted this farce and agreed to work with K on the whitewash.

After a week in his new job, however, Kissinger resigned rather than reveal the names of his Kissinger and Associates business clients—among them were thought to be Saudi Arabian royalty with close connections to those suspected of bankrolling the 9/11 terrorists. Well, K knows his priorities:

profits before politics—or anything. Too bad, I thought. I would have looked forward to reading the equivalent of the Warren Commission Report on 9/11. I guess I'll have to wait for the next sick joke emanating from George W. Bush's cheerleading mind!

THE BUSH VISION AND THE CULTURE OF POWER[*]

George W. Bush arose from a culture, not a Petri dish with putrid algae, but one that blended an upper-class sense of self-worth, shared by mostly worthless people, with another upper-class notion that God rewarded those who have wealth and meant the rest to suffer.

The head of a large empire needs a world vision, some sense that he knows that his policies coincide with the future, a road map that takes us beyond 'they hate us' and 'we love freedom.' President Bush's post-9/11 speeches, remarks at infrequent press conferences and occasional off-the-cuff quips, however, don't offer much clarity about how he sees the coincidence between his policies and, say, the future of the environment or the fate of more than half the world's desperately poor people, factors one must consider when thinking reasonably about the future.

I have observed, in the seemingly interminable period of time since the Supreme Court selected him, some evolution in W's behavior. From a rather crude and simplistic view of the world as Texas Governor, he has built on his old prejudices and added a few new twists. In his new mutation as imperial manager, for example, criminals have come to play a crucial role in this Texas–Yale *Weltanschauung.*

As Governor of Texas, Bush didn't believe in rehabilitating criminals. Indeed, those on death row didn't benefit from his compassionate conservatism. In fact, as governor for five years he presided over 152 killings, more executions than any other state leader.[39] In his June 17, 2000 column in the *New York Times*, Anthony Lewis quotes a February 2000 speech by Bush in which he proclaimed his confidence 'that every person that has been put to death in Texas under my watch has been guilty of the crime charged, and has had full access to the courts.'

As Anthony Lewis noted, however, in one-third of those cases, the report showed that the lawyer who represented the death penalty defendant at trial or on appeal had been or was later disbarred or otherwise sanctioned. In

*   Originally appeared in *Progreso Weekly*, December 12, 2002, and later in *CounterPunch*. I watched a rerun of an old President George W. Bush speech and instead of throwing up I decided to write something.

40 cases the lawyers presented no evidence at all or only one witness at the sentencing phase of the trial. In almost 30 other cases, prosecutors used psychiatric testimony based on experts who had not bothered to even interview the people on trial for their lives.

Bush dismissed serious studies that raised doubts about the death penalty, even brushing aside reservations held by such staunch advocates of capital punishment as the Taliban-like Pat Robertson. 'We've adequately answered innocence or guilt,' Bush declared smugly to an *Associated Press* reporter. He assured reporters that every defendant 'had full access to a fair trial.' He also ignored the Illinois Republican Governor George Ryan's serious study of the death penalty, which found that police had tortured confessions out of more than a dozen people and that serious flaws had occurred in the trials and police procedures of other men waiting on death row.

As with much of policy, Bush doesn't rely on facts, especially when life and death are involved. His instinct tells him that when dealing with difficulty, whether on policy toward terrorism, war with Iraq or the death penalty, think of a joke. When Tucker Carlson asked him how he felt about putting a woman to death in a September 2000 *Talk* magazine interview, W mimicked her plea to save her. '"Please," Bush whimpers,' wrote Carlson describing his demeanor as his lips pursed in mock desperation, '"don't kill me."'

As President, Bush has apparently reconsidered his stance on criminals, well, certain kinds anyway. His new rehabilitation program calls for the appointment to high policy posts of former felons who have links to mass murder, not just simple homicide. These lawbreakers have also shown their utter contempt for the lives of Central Americans, the US Congress and Constitution as well.

Take as examples officials he recently named to manage important policy positions: Elliot Abrams, appointed to the National Security Council; John Poindexter, head of the Information Awareness Office; John Negroponte, the Permanent US Representative to the UN; and Otto Reich, a Latin America envoy.

These four characters conspired to circumvent Congress in the 1980s. Because the CIA-backed Contras had committed human rights violations and blatant acts of terrorism, Congress defunded them in 1985. In 1981, President Reagan had chosen the universally discredited Contras to depose the leftist government of Nicaragua. The kill-crazy Contras, however, had acquired serious admirers in Washington, including the four above mentioned characters. These high-laced conspirators decided to sell missiles to Iran (also prohibited by Congress) so that they could funnel the proceeds to their beloved Contras, and then cover it up.

In his testimony to Congress, the scrappy Abrams made witness history when he declared: 'I never said I had no idea about most of the things you said I had no idea about.' The now 54-year-old Abrams also explained in his autobiography that he had to inform his young children about the headline announcing his indictment, so he told them he had to lie to Congress to protect the national interest.[40]

The then Deputy Assistant Secretary of State to Central America pleaded guilty to withholding information from Congress and received two years' probation and 100 hours' community work. Now, the 'pardoned' Abrams as the new White House man on the Middle East, having learned that one can get away with felonious behavior if one maintains close links to the Bush family, will attempt to redraw the roadmap of the Middle East. The Secretary of State, Colin Powell, drafted a plan for designing a peaceful solution and eventually a Palestinian state. The vision, by deduction, amounts to a rubber stamp for Israeli repression and expansion. It also coincides with Abrams stated belief that Israel and the United States will benefit from tighter connections with the far right fundamentalist Christians who want Israel to prevail and occupy all of Palestine and US policy.

Former retired admiral and national security adviser to Reagan John Poindexter was convicted of five felonies involving conspiracy, obstruction of Congress, and making false statements. The judge gave him six months in prison, but an appellate court reversed the sentence because Congress had previously granted him immunity. His slipping out of prison on a procedural error does not change the facts of the case. Poindexter's vision runs toward secrecy and circumventing law. In his latest declaration, he assures the public that the privacy of individuals is not affiliated with terrorism.

Otto Reich ran Latin America policy until November 2002 and now holds a special appointment from the White House for Latin America. Critics called Reich the Minister of Lying, an appropriate title for his previous post as Reagan's head of the Office of Public Diplomacy and less than artful cover-ups of human rights violations by the Contras.

Negroponte, now Ambassador to the UN, also played the Iran-Contra game, covering up human rights abuses by 'our' military friends in Honduras and narrowly escaping indictment. What liberal critics called human rights abuse, Reich and Negroponte understood as necessary for US national security—you can't make an omelet without breaking the eggs, or some such Maoism.

By appointing these characters, W's world view becomes clearer. Those who participated in Central American plots that caused the deaths of tens of thousands will have a second chance to show the public what they really stand for. Indeed, they remain as role models for the United States in its post-republican incarnation.

Congress has little place in such an imperial government. The media, epitomized by *Fox News* and Rupert Murdoch's chains, pushes the Bush crowd's aggressive war game and simultaneously diverts the public with the trivialities of everyday 'reality television.'

The National Security Plan released by the White House in September 2002 further shreds the republican fabric by placing the Bill of Rights into second-class status in its search for 'full spectral dominance,' hardly a plan that relates to the Republic or security for that matter.

In this imperial obsession, gone also are past notions of accountability and openness, when administrations felt it necessary to at least try to cover imperial expeditions with vestiges of republican organs.

The Bush vision promotes unashamedly the American way of life, one shared by majorities in Western Europe, Japan, Australia and New Zealand. For W, this means that leisure, pleasure, and relaxation, based on the individual's freedom to buy commodities, will presumably satisfy any and all reasonable human urges. Implicit in this paradigm is God's reward for the wealthy in the United States, who shouldn't pay any taxes. God holds out a promise for the rest of the world: they too can succeed by adopting the American set of values.

The US government under this image exercises naked imperial power to bring non-compliant nations into the global corporate model under the guise of saving the world from terrorists and drug traffickers, making everything more democratic and, of course, protecting our interests—which are usually 'classified.'

The few dissenters to this overarching scheme demand changes in Middle East policy that reflect regional realities and notions of equality and justice, and feel vulnerable to attacks on their patriotism. Those who focus on the immediate needs of the impoverished 3 billion plus people, and the screaming demands of the environment, where the ice melting phenomenon has scientists truly concerned, just don't understand the culture of power.

In Bush's mind, power derives from the assumption that God has placed Nature in man's path for his immediate and perpetual use. Trees are for chopping down for packing crates, tooth picks, paper and furniture, of course; animals are to kill for meat, hide and sport; fish to catch; land to develop and drill on and so forth. Those who refer to income gaps incite 'class warfare.' However mad it may seem, this vision symbolizes the nature of the people who currently manipulate power and wealth.

Their logic of power reigns as a cultural imperative. This world view eschews consequences. The White House insiders smirk at references to increasing global poverty or ecological decay and quote irrelevant biblical passages—as if somehow God justifies their lust for his power.

Bush relates to men who exercise power without thought, like the Israeli Prime Minister, Ariel Sharon, whom he called 'a man of peace,' and members of the Saudi royal family. Sharon's vision of a greater Israel coincides with the views of Bush's theological supporters, like the reverends Jerry Falwell and Pat Robertson, whose biblical mumbo-jumbo demands that Israel conquer the Middle East. The oily Saudis literally fuel the imperial drive.

The logic of naked imperial power also includes a world of bizarre contrasts. As Wade Davis underlines in the July 6, 2002 *Globe and Mail*, Americans spend as much on lawn maintenance as the government of India collects in federal tax revenue. The Bush vision of a world under the thumb of US power requires a $400 billion defense budget, larger than the entire economy of Australia. Yet, more than one sixth of the world's population exists on less than $1 a day.

When Bush asked in his September 20, 2001 address to Congress, 'Why do they hate us?' I understood that he could not imagine how playing video golf or shaking hands with a six-foot rat at Disneyland could offend other people. Bush grew up with commercial values—and alcohol—and knows only one notion of development. He seems unable to understand that his model has failed in the Middle East and throughout the Third World.

Those who have followed its commands did not realize prosperity and happiness.

The model, based on high consumption of energy and other resources that damage the environment, does not coincide with the realities of Nature. Bush's vision of power and the facts of earth are on a collision course.

He assumes that science and technology, the cause of some of the acute problems, can solve whatever issues arise. Look how many babies now live that once would have perished. The whole world enjoys increased life expectancy, but if one looks deeper into the kind of lives that Third World people lead, one sees something that obviously escapes George W's vision. An Asian garment worker sewing jeans for The Gap makes about $88 a month.[41] That is, he literally falls into the gap, as The Gap's advertisement inadvertently tells us.

That gap has nothing to do with fashion modes. Rather, as Davis describes, it means families of six share one bed in one room off a warren of alleys strewn with human waste and refuse.

The majority of the world will not share in Bush's world. Nor does he envision them participating. Bush's vision presumes that the majority of the world's people can and will forget the past. What had been traditional values, languages and customs will be absorbed inside the commodity culture, the only one he can imagine, and from which his vision of power has emerged. That power rests on immense wealth and military potency.

What the innocent Americans have learned through 9/11, however, is that neither their government's wealth nor military power translates into security. America can continue to export *Baywatch* into remote hamlets throughout the Middle East, but that will not stop the melting of polar ice caps, the warming of the globe or the rising of the ocean levels, nor will it touch the scourge of poverty.

Likewise, anti-Americanism will spread. The December 5, 2002 *Los Angeles Times* describes a recent Pew Research Center for the People and the Press public opinion study in 44 countries. Called *What the World Thinks in 2002,* the report found anti-American sentiment in Muslim countries to be profound. The problems that concern the world's majority, according to the report, include the gap between rich and poor, hunger, the environment and AIDS. Ironically, the majority in countries like Egypt and Turkey like 'American technology and culture [but] they are displeased over the spread of American ideas.' Here ideas mean not just the exporting of *Baywatch* and other T&A shows, but refer also to the exercise of naked imperial power in the Middle East.

Under Bush, working with others has meant bowing and scraping to the ultra right, subservience to the gun and anti-abortion lobbies, and carte blanche for the anti-Castro Cuban terrorists who helped elect him. Ironically, only criminal methods can realize W's world vision. His culture of power means a government of men, not laws, willing to subjugate, dominate, and impose their will on people and nature. And if you can't think of a good answer for a pesky reporter, tell a joke.

If you agree with this analysis then you'll conclude, as I have, that we face a dangerous situation and you will thus be motivated to get off your ass and do something about it.

Part III

Between Iraq and a Hard Place: The Oily Empire Stomps Through the Middle East

Because the United States entered the imperial race long after the European empires had established their strategies, it never formulated a coherent Middle East policy. After World War II, the State Department supported most of the corrupt Arab rulers and their undemocratic systems as the simplest means of maintaining regional equilibrium and control of the vital oil supply. Then, as the 1948 election campaign developed and polls showed the Republican Thomas Dewey defeating Harry S. Truman, who had ascended to the presidency after Franklin Roosevelt died in 1945, Clark Clifford proposed a shocking change. Clifford, a young lawyer and Truman adviser, who later emerged as a kind of kingmaker in the Democratic Party, suggested that to win the election Truman must switch US Middle East policy to support the new state of Israel and thus capture both the Jewish vote (New York had the largest number of electoral votes and the largest Jewish population) and enlist the support of Jewish media owners and practitioners. The underdog Truman, disregarding protests from the State Department and the navy, followed Clifford's counsel, got the support he needed and won the election.

His victory also showed some Jewish leaders their potential power in US politics. Before a decade had passed the Israeli lobby had formed.[42] It grew in influence to become the single most influential foreign policy pressure group in modern history.

Because of the lobby's power, Congress began to reward Israel with yearly handouts of billions of dollars and loans. The Pentagon shared some of its military technology and secrets with Israel's Defense Forces. By the late 1960s, the media portrayed Israelis as virtuous democrats; Palestinians as undeserving terrorists. The national security mavens had figured out a formula to support Israel and protect US control of the Middle East.

Romance corrupt but oily and compliant Arab dictatorships; characterize the disobedient ones as evil.

But the formula did not ameliorate the core struggle. It has become impossible to discuss the Middle East or US policy in the region without referring to the Israeli–Palestinian conflict. Indeed, the Israel–Palestine debacle looms like a specter of darkness over the world. And Judaism, the religion—the ethic of a people that has survived thousands of years of persecution and a Holocaust—is also threatened by that conflict.

FACE FACTS: ISRAEL IS LOSING A WAR AND HER ETHICS[*]

After the creation of the Jewish state in 1948, following in the wake of Nazi atrocities against Jews, some Israelis believed that Jews and Palestinians could—indeed would have to—share the same small piece of land and thus live together in peace. Extremists, however, thought they could expel the Palestinians, or make life so miserable for them that they would have to leave. Millions of Palestinians did flee or were informally expelled. But millions remained. Irresponsible heads of neighboring Arab states also played a bellicose role in the early conflict, encouraging war against Israel and then refusing to take in many of the Palestinian refugees. Some Arab leaders used the 'push them into the sea' slogan to inspire Arabs against Jews, words beyond inappropriate after the experience of the Holocaust.

The extremists on both sides have endured and reproduced. The Palestinian crazies program suicide bombers and repeat their insane slogan. But the Jewish fanatics have state power. Almost 55 years after the birth of Israel, the Prime Minister, Ariel Sharon, retains his youthful conviction that, by increasing Palestinian suffering, in some not too distant future he can either force them to surrender any claims to independence and sovereignty and move them into Bantustan-like territories or make their lives so uncomfortable they will leave.

Unlike the framing of the issue by US-based pro-Israel groups, who claim to represent all mainstream American Jews, the current Middle East bloodbath has nothing to do with Israeli survival or with supposed plans by the Palestinian leader, Yasser Arafat, to drive the Jews into the sea (he doesn't use that slogan). Quite the opposite! Sharon has convinced his backers at

---

[*]   Originally appeared in *Progreso Weekly*, March 28, 2002. A spate of Palestinian suicide bombings, followed by Israeli retaliatory attacks, continued to prevail throughout March 2002. This lingering reality overshadowed the March 27–28, 2002 Arab League Summit (Palestinian leader Yasser Arafat was banned from attending), in which Crown Prince Abdullah announced the Saudi Peace Plan.

home and abroad that Israel should deploy its military to accomplish the task that should have been completed in the 1940s: expel the Palestinians.

In 1982 Sharon, then Defense Minister, tried to 'solve' the 'Palestinian problem' by orchestrating the Israeli invasion of Lebanon, where the Palestine Liberation Organization (PLO) had made its headquarters. As part of that operation, according to the 1983 Israeli Kahan Commission which investigated the affair, Sharon played a key role in the massacre at the Sabra and Shatila Palestinian refugee camps in Lebanon during which pro-Israeli Lebanese paramilitary forces under Sharon's orders murdered some 1,200 refugees. As Prime Minister, Sharon denies his role in these slaughters, but insists that the Israeli military will attain its historic goal and rid the historic territory of Palestine of Palestinians.[43]

TV and newspaper reports about the Palestinian response to increased military assaults, however, appear to contradict the very foundations of Sharon's strategy. Instead of yielding to the power of Israeli tanks blasting away with cannons and machine guns and F-15s firing rockets at civilian targets in West Bank and Gaza cities and refugee camps, the Palestinians appear to have increased their will to resist.

Ironically, the US mass media tends to repeat Sharon's mantra by using the Israeli euphemism 'terrorists' to describe an occupied people and their plight. The talking television heads invariably repeat Bush's pejorative patter about Arafat—who, in fact, because of Israel's military power cannot control his own fate—failing to stop the psychotic practice of Hamas and other fanatics who recruit and send suicide bombers to Israel.

The military barrage, the inability of people to work, or obtain food and water, attend schools or have access to hospitals and electricity have hardened the very backbone of the people they were supposed to soften. Indeed, hundreds if not thousands of Palestinians have declared themselves ready to die and even commit suicide for their cause, and there is reason to believe that Sharon's display of naked military power has only increased the number of potential suicide bombers and resistance fighters.

This fact, of course, raises the uncomfortable but logical question: why threaten people with death if they have already volunteered to die? On the Israeli side, few, I think, would undertake certain death missions. As Israeli writer and war veteran Uri Avnery writes: 'Palestinians know full well that they are fighting for their very existence; Israelis know that they are fighting for the settlements and bankrupt politicians.'[44] He refers to the settlements continuously built in the midst of occupied Palestinian land, in defiance of the 1993 Oslo Peace Accords.[45]

Sharon's strategy threatens Israel's fragile sense of cohesion and its western way of life. Israelis avoid going to the movies, cafes, or theaters; they stay home, fearing suicide bombers. Israeli parents with kids in the military worry that they will not return home alive or in one piece. 'Will it be my son's tank that hits the land mine?' And for how long must this continue?

Journalists quote Israelis who feel queasy about the images they see on TV, about how their military behaves with a civilian population. They have not all become hardened to images of Israeli bulldozers destroying the homes of those who supposedly have terrorists in their families while Palestinian women and children weep in the background. And some Israelis who do not chant slogans like 'Kill all Arabs'—or think that way—have begun to have serious qualms about a 'war' in which their soldiers react to stone throwing teenagers by firing missiles from jets and helicopter gunships.

Sharon has even invited TV photographers to capture images at a Palestinian refugee camp of Israelis brutalizing their captives. The Israeli news shows hundreds of young to middle-aged Palestinian men with their wrists locked in handcuffs, blindfolds covering their eyes. Heavily armed Israeli troops then push them toward an 'interrogation center.'

Palestinian children watch their fathers and older brothers bound, blindfolded and occasionally spat on by uniformed Israelis. Reporters simply refer to these places occupied by Israeli armed forces as 'refugee camps.' They don't report that many of the families in these sordid locations have lived there since 1948 when the Israelis drove them from their homes.

Do the majority of Israelis see these images positively? Outside of his right-wing constituency, which has always backed his expel-the-Arabs stance, Sharon emerges as a dangerous man, a loose cannon—albeit, in the minds of many Israelis, a necessary one for this harsh time.

But, in Washington, even some of Israel's most uncritical supporters are beginning to see Israeli behavior as a liability to US future plans to pursue Al-Qaeda, bomb Iraq and extend the 'war against terrorism' to still other parts of the Muslim world. President Bush, after much of the Arab world demonstrated in the streets and even European leaders—usually docile—pressed him, finally asked Sharon to withdraw Israeli forces from Palestinian territories. His solemn voice reminded me, however, of the parent supposedly clamping down on his kid after years of indiscipline. It was Bush saying to his ally (child): 'Go to your room—at your earliest convenience.'

Sharon has miscalculated how much he could get away with as well as the impact of his policy to isolate the Palestinian leader. By demonstrating that he could virtually imprison Arafat in his own home, he showed the weakness of the Palestinian Authority; but in the world of public opinion Sharon also rescued a failed leader who was heading toward the scrap heap of history. Palestinians, according to their own polls, had begun to tire of Arafat's bumbling over the decades. Now, thanks to Sharon's heavy handedness, Arafat has emerged as an old man who shares the suffering of all Palestinians at the hands of the Israeli occupiers.

Israelis have paid a heavy national price for occupying Palestinian land. As the Israeli death toll mounts and as Palestinian deaths and suffering reach new heights, the stain on Israel's image abroad spreads as well. Ads denouncing Sharon's tactics have appeared in prestigious US newspapers and each day I receive email appeals from different Jewish groups to protest against the outrageous and immoral behavior of the Israeli government. More than 1,500 have died in this short war between a powerful Israeli military and Palestinian civilians or suicide bombers and resistance fighters.

The United States, which has treated Israel as the most special of all its allies, lavishing it with aid and military equipment, now can pursue its own interests by stopping Sharon's aggressive behavior and supporting the peace plan proposed by Saudi Arabia's Crown Prince Abdullah at the March 2002 Arab League Summit in Beirut. Under this plan, the Arab world would recognize Israel and establish normal relations with it, in return for Israel's recognition of clear boundaries (pre-1967) and a Palestinian state. It sounds reasonable and just. But as Avnery points out: 'Thirty-five years of occupation and settlement have eroded Israel's ability to reason, leaving instead a mixture of arrogance and folly.'[46]

Jewish theologian Marc Ellis of Baylor University agrees. Israelis have become so warlike, he thinks, that they should 'replace the Torah and Ark of the Covenant in the synagogue with a liturgical representation of a helicopter gunship.' Until Israel began to demand that its soldiers act like occupiers, usurp other people's land, raze houses, and assassinate individuals, there existed a unique Jewish ethic, a code of conduct that defined justice and equity for Jewish people. Thanks to Israeli policies, Ellis argues, that special conscience that has endured for a millennium, has nearly vanished.[47]

Perhaps, I think, Israelis can save their souls and get peace in their land if they stop the war, end the occupation and treat the Saudi peace plan seriously, not just as another blueprint they can circumvent as they have all previous plans, but as a chance to save a great people's ethic, the essence of Judaism. Once Sharon and his nasty and hateful ideologues leave the seat of power, it should not take a Sherlock Holmes to figure out that Jews and Palestinians will eventually have to share this land and to do so they must establish a way of living together—in peace.

A big 'if' remains in the Israeli–Palestinian issue. If Hamas and the other fanatic elements can stop sending suicide bombers into Israel, the Palestinian people will likely benefit from the divisions within Israel. More Palestinian violence will only strengthen Sharon and the hardliners and create

temporary unity among Israelis of diverse views. No one should under-
estimate the absence of strategic thinking from these sectors of Palestinian
leadership. But only a fool employs violence against a better-armed enemy
and pursues tactics that will unify that foe as well.

ISRAELI ORTHODOX MISSIONARIES RECRUIT IN PERU[*]

*Israelis tell the story of a rabbi fervently praying at the Wailing Wall and a tourist
who sees him and takes some video footage of this dramatic scene. The rabbi stops
and the tourist apologizes:*

*'Forgive me, Rabbi, but I couldn't resist filming such energetic prayer. What were
you praying for?'*

*'I was praying that the Jews and Palestinians would stop this crazy fighting and
live in peace with each other,' says the Rabbi.*

*'Wow,' says the tourist, 'what a great theme. Do you think you were getting
anywhere with your prayers?'*

'Feh,' says the rabbi, 'it's like talking to the wall.'

Religious Jews, like Christians, believe in the Messiah, the Savior God will
send to earth to usher in the era of world peace and redemption. But most
Jews don't hold their breath. Indeed, a traditional Jewish gag tells of a poor
Jew who agrees to a small salary to sit just outside the town's entrance so
he can greet the Messiah and then inform the rest.

'Why,' asks the man's wife critically, 'would you accept such low wages?'

'Well, it doesn't pay much, but it's a steady job,' replies the man.

Some contemporary Orthodox rabbis, who recently challenged the
religious legitimacy of non-orthodox Jews, have apparently lost their
traditional sense of humor; or, they have turned downright zany. Fearful
that there no longer exists a sufficient Jewish population in the world with
which to complete the settlement of Palestinian territories, some rabbis
decided on a recruitment plan that runs directly counter to Jewish law,
which strongly discourages proselytizing. Indeed, Jewish law mandates the
rabbi to discourage conversion. The rabbi must probe unnervingly into the
hopeful convert's motives, challenge him with life-long obstacles that he'll
likely encounter by becoming Jewish.

---

[*] Originally appeared in *Progreso Weekly*, July 31, 2002. I read in *Ha'aretz* that Israeli
Orthodox rabbis had gone to Peru to recruit recently converted Inca descendents to
settle the West Bank and serve in the Israeli Defense Forces.

Nonetheless, the Chief Orthodox Rabbi of Israel has dispatched a rabbinical delegation of missionaries to Peru, of all places, to find converts. But—here's the catch—in order to qualify for conversion—and thus the right to live in Israel—those Peruvians must agree to settle inside the Occupied Territories.

A July 19, 2002 Israeli *Ha'aretz* article reports that the rabbis sent to Peru by Chief Rabbi Israel Meir Lau had indeed converted a group of impoverished descendents of the Incas, to become pioneers of Zion on Palestinian territory. The reporter Neri Livneh quotes Rabbi Eliyahu Birnbaum, a judge in the Israeli Conversion Court and a member of the delegation, who described how the rabbis traveled to the Peruvian hinterland and brought their recruits to Lima 'to be immersed in the ocean. Then we also had to remarry them all in a Jewish ceremony according to the *halakha* [Jewish religious law].' To convert from Catholicism to Judaism, the rabbis stressed, the Peruvians had to immediately relocate to Israel.

After that, came a piece of rabbinical logic that could only derive from blind fanaticism or a parody of Solomon Simon's *Wise Men of Helm*, the fools who believed passionately in nonsense, which they then labeled wisdom.

Rabbi David Mamo, the Deputy President of the Conversion Court, told *Ha'aretz* that the rabbis made converts first go to Lima 'because in the remote areas where they live, there is no possibility of keeping kosher and it was important for us to ensure that they would live in a Jewish environment.' Noting apparently an astonished look on the reporter's face, Mamo went further: 'In fact, there was no need for the condition because they were in any case imbued with a love of the Land of Israel in a way that is hard to describe.'

One rabbi who spoke Spanish said he was astonished to see 'real Indians who wanted to convert to Judaism, but then I saw that they were strong in their faith and that they observe the commandments. They are very simple but good-hearted people with a powerful spirit and after examining the matter we decided to convert them. However, we did not convert all of them, only those we saw as serious and who said they were willing to "go up" [emigrate] to the Land of Israel.'

Rabbi Birnbaum added that after he saw their enthusiasm for the Land of Israel, 'we understood that conversion was part of a complete process including *aliyah* [emigration to Israel], so we told them: "Just as you live in a community here, you should join a community in Israel, too."'

But not just any community! The 90 Peruvians went straight from the Tel Aviv airport to new settlements in the West Bank with the blessing of the Jewish agency responsible for making sure Jews from western countries get to settle in Israel. The agency Director said that if the rabbis put the kosher stamp on converting Peruvian Jews, who was she to object?

Ha'aretz asked Rabbi Birnbaum why he didn't ask the newly converted Peruvians to simply become part of the existing Peruvian Jewish community.

'How can I put it without hurting anyone?' Birnbaum replied. 'The community in Lima consists of a certain socioeconomic class and did not want them because they are from a lower level. There was a kind of agreement that if they were converted, they would not join the Lima community, so there was no choice but to lay down the condition that they emigrate to Israel.'

Two weeks earlier Efrain Perez, then known as Nilo, lived in the town of Trujillo and knew little of Israel or world geography. 'Now, thank God,' he told reporter Livneh, 'we live where the patriarch, Abraham, the number one Jew, roamed.'

'We are of Indian origin,' says Nachshon Ben-Haim, formerly Pedro Mendosa, 'but in Peru, in the Andes, there is no Indian culture left. Everyone has become Christian, and before we became Jews, we also were Christians who went to church.'

Ben-Haim wants to join the army after finishing his Hebrew course, 'because I wasn't in the army in Peru and that is something I lack, and also because I want to defend the country and if there is no choice, I will kill Arabs. But I am sure that Jews kill Arabs only for self-defense and justice, but Arabs do it because they like to kill.'

Livneh reports that the recently converted Peruvian explained his scientific view of Judaism: 'the Arab has the instinct of murder and killing like all gentiles, and only Jews do not have that instinct—that is a genetic fact.'

Brainwashing? My grandmother, not an educated woman, used to cover my eyes when a nun wearing her habit would pass on the street. 'Evil eye,' she would mutter, along with some mantra in Yiddish. Superstition flourishes among the ignorant. Those missionaries who promise material wealth like free land and housing to impoverished Latin Americans naturally find conversion of poor people much easier than the Jehovah's Witnesses who offer them nothing but their peculiar road to God's truth.

Solomon Simon's wise men of Helm might have scratched their heads in wonder at the chutzpah of the Orthodox rabbis traveling to Inca country to recruit for their expansionist cause. And, inventing dogma to justify it! Like the Helm sages, the orthodox missionaries to Peru utilized bizarre logic to arrive at the convenient solution. Unlike the naïve sages of Helm, however, the Orthodox rabbis colored supposed religious scruples with irrational dreams of an expanded Israel, populated by, well, whomever they might designate as Jewish. So, Peruvian Jews now immerse themselves in Hebrew studies on Palestinian land and pick up army rifles to kill Palestinians, people they had barely heard of a few months ago.

You can laugh at the idiocy of their logic, or that of other newly arrived settlers who expound equally outlandish doctrines.

This story should encourage people interested in Middle East peace to learn more about the daily reality of that area of conflict. Perhaps we might demand that western media moguls stop acting like morons from Helm and proclaim in their headlines and TV leads: 'It's the occupation, stupid! Stop it now and the peace process can move forward!'

Is this like talking to the wall?

Part IV

Latin America: The Imperial Economic Model, Obedience and Terrorism

The move to 'globalize' has meant turning parts of 'underdeveloped' Third World countries into integrated pieces in the global production–distribution–consumption pattern: progress. This process has meant yet another industrial revolution. In China, as many as 300 million peasants have had to leave the countryside over the last three decades. Tens of millions of these former country people now operate factory machines in polluted cities located along the eastern coast, where they provide a substantial percentage of world production in items ranging from cheap low-tech products to very high-end, high-tech machinery. In other countries this urbanization process has involved less dramatic numbers. But the rapid cultural turnaround that results from such a dislocated population has occurred in dozens of Third World countries.

In Mexico, since the 1960s, perhaps as many as 30 million people have found their ways from the land to cities where they work in the maquilas. While factory workers in now burgeoning industrial centers like Tijuana or Juarez belong to a world-wide urban proletariat culture, linked by their common relationship to production, they also have a special link to US culture. It is not just the cultural infection of McDonald's, but the long-standing pattern of US domination, indeed intervention, of Latin America that continues to prevail on the political as well as the economic front.

Since the onset of its successful 1959 revolution, the Cuban government has resisted US controls on all levels. This has made Cuba 'special.' In this section, I offer some on-the-scene observations and reflections about how socialist Cuba has survived in the post-Soviet sea of globalization.

Except for Cuba and a few other holdouts, globalization has meant the accelerated transference of US commercial culture and the ideology of the free market as the best of all systems. Thus far, that system has not provided

Latin Americans or most other Third World people with the benefits that its proponents, the neo-liberal free trade ideologues represented in institutions like the IMF, World Bank and the Harvard School of Business, have touted. Indeed, Latin Americans in several countries recently responded to the conditions of life under free market capitalism by electing opponents of that system.[48] In Venezuela, the United States backed an April 2002 coup to oust the nation's democratically elected leader, Hugo Chavez.

Latin Americans have also recently discovered that the US war on terrorism relates also to economic and political relations with the United States. The US Trade Representative, Robert 'Zealous' Zoellick, deemed fast track (giving the President power to negotiate broad trade agreements like NAFTA subject only to a yes-or-no vote by Congress) an essential tool as a means of fighting terrorism. He appealed to the fear that the United States will be further paralyzed if Bush is not granted fast track trade power,[49] as he tried to intimidate the few opposing voices in Congress. Cooperating non-terrorist countries would get rewarded with access to rich foreign markets.

CAPITALISM WAVES THE FLAG AND THE RULES[*]

Just as gunboat diplomacy was linked to dollar diplomacy as a means of securing US interests in the early decades of the twentieth century, so too does the policy of coup making and terrorism link to US economic policy in the early twenty-first century. In their promotion material, however, the purveyors of 'neo-liberalism' omit explanations of such details. Nor do they elaborate on how the model itself was constructed: on theft, corruption and shady dealing, the very practices that the free marketers now decry as deadly sins in Latin America. So, to understand how Latin Americans might begin their orientation course on the American economic model, a brief survey of the US wealthy class and their ancestors might prove enlightening.

Soviet socialism died about eleven years ago and capitalism's major advocates basked in victory and declared as the best of all possible their reigning economic model. I call this model *opulenics*: the economic theory— or self-justification ethos—designed by those living in opulence.

Cruise the well-separated mansions of Rancho Santa Fe, California, the East Hamptons on New York's Long Island or the lush estates of West Palm Beach, Florida and their equivalents in hundreds of other locations and

---

*   Originally appeared in *Progreso Weekly*, July 11, 2002. I lost a quarter of my pension savings ($10,000) when WorldCom declared bankruptcy.

you'll understand that hundreds of thousands of Americans have accumulated humongous portions of the world's wealth. The massive garages of these modern manors shelter numerous cars, each one of which costs many times what a Bangladeshi earns in several lifetimes; in the closets and drawers, clothing and jewelry that would account for several more lifetimes of labor for a Third World family.

The accumulation of wealth by theft and fraud, however, is steeped in American tradition. Long before the nineteenth-century Robber Baron era, the Founding Father Benjamin Franklin had a scam with his son-in-law to buy arms and uniforms at reduced prices in Paris for George Washington's revolutionary army. The son-in-law then sold them at full market price to the Continental Congress. The Rockefeller, Carnegie, Mellon and Vanderbilt seniors, who barely stayed on the windy side of the law to build their vast fortunes, hired public relations flacks to brighten their larcenous images. Later, academic lackeys renamed them industrial statesmen. Their modern equivalents, like the CEOs of Enron and WorldCom, continued in that tradition. These well-paid executives carried out massive fraud on shareholders and consumers alike, in collusion with their accountants. They won endorsements from those in political power.

Once lionized by President Bush himself as the very pillars of contemporary ethics, these CEO Republican stalwarts have now shown at least one other side of their character. So brazen was their larceny that their good friend W had to promise to punish for criminal business practices the 'good buddies' who secured his election with large contributions. The same oil and gas executives had plotted with Cheney, the Vice President, on a supersecret counsel to work out the 2001 National Energy Plan.

Now that the public has learned that these super-rich hustlers had only disguised themselves as the gentry and trustees of our society, the President pretends he hardly knew them. Indeed, W can barely recall any association with Enron's former CEO Kenneth Lay, a man who dropped a sizeable fortune into the Bush presidential campaign.

So, understand the scandals against the backdrop of euphemisms like 'free trade,' 'globalization,' 'neo-liberalism' and the 'free market.' Do not let them fool you about the character of the ruling economic system.

We have learned that the CEOs of companies worth many hundreds of billions of dollars have lied to and screwed their stockholders and stolen money from consumers. But they had begun their public pickpocketing activities long before the Enron executives, for example, rigged legislation and connived at federal appointments, which allowed them to filch billions from California energy users in 2001. They secretly sold their own stock in the company when the trouble began to become apparent while forbidding their employees to sell theirs. Until they got caught, they conspired with auditors and bankers while encouraging unsuspecting citizens to invest their pension funds in Enron stocks—with the overt blessings of the nation's First Family.

Now, the workers of these corporations have lost their jobs, their savings and their faith. Some of those California consumers bilked by corporate fraud can barely pay their gas and electric bills as they read that Pacific Gas and Electric Company executives paid themselves lucrative bonuses just before they declared bankruptcy.

Meanwhile, democracy, the system that supposedly dovetails into the prevailing free-market economic system, has become less than functional in many parts of the world. 'Electionism' might better describe a system where candidates who agree 100 per cent on national economic policies vie for political power. Like US politicians, they appear on television and cast aspersions on each other's characters. This is US democracy operating in Colombia, for example.

If democracy means rule by the majority, we face an odd contradiction. In the United States the majority have not voted for decades. Or, taken positively, they vote for none of the above. Yet, Bush demands the US style of democracy in a region where the majority of nations, including the US's close allies don't even possess a façade of republican government. Bush's good buddy Saudi Crown Prince Abdullah was elected by virtue of a lucky sperm cell. His even more corrupt Kuwaiti neighbors, whose butts George I saved, have as much respect for democracy as the fox does for the chickens.

In 2002, Bush II served as the prime salesman for both the economic and political systems that have failed the vast majority of the world's population. Imagine, on June 25, WorldCom—after declaring unbelievably great growth rates in 1999 and 2000—announced that it had mis-recorded $3.8 billion in costs, a sum that pushed the company to bankruptcy's brink. The CEOs of other communication giants blamed the catastrophe on competition, the very dynamic that supposedly makes the system run smoothly.

But, as the old monopolists said back in the early twentieth century: 'competition is war and war is Hell.' So, William T. Esrey, Sprint's Chief Executive, told a *New York Times Money and Business* reporter in a June 30, 2002 story that competition in the 1990s had grown into 'price wars' that had 'decimated the long distance industry.' This level of real competition he called an 'unsustainable, almost irrational' (note the almost) pursuit of growth.

But if competition is supposed to make system run correctly and that leads to war, what does drive the American system? Periodically, in the past, the big moguls engaged in hanky-panky schemes in which they linked their financial windfalls to the purchase of powerful political mountebanks.

In the late nineteenth century, The French Mississippi Company swindled millions of stockholders as did a variety of similar British schemes. Like the US Teapot Dome scandal of the 1920s[50] and similar frauds throughout US history, these shenanigans invariably involve cases of businessmen funding politicians who, in turn, grant the sleazy corporate executives the favors they need to run the scam.

Is this what democracy means in practice? Occasionally, the people, in rage and anger over the levels of injustice, take to the streets or demonstrate their extreme unhappiness with the system at the voting booth. In street protests, the police beat them up and jail them. Judges sentence them. But, if they keep coming back, sometimes they can win a few reforms—or get put away for longer sentences.

But reforms don't endure, as the Enron example shows. Enron simply bought the Texan Senator Phil Gramm and his wife Wendy, and other high-placed Republicans and Democrats who did their administrative and legislative bidding. Wendy Gramm sanctioned the exemption in trading of energy derivatives while serving under Bush I as chair of the Commodity Futures Trading Commission. Soon after, she resigned from her government position and became an Enron board member. Senator Gramm had accumulated $97,350 in political contributions from Enron since 1990.[51]

This system promoted by US advertisers and public relations spin doctors as the best ever devised, indeed the only way to deal with economy and politics, has excluded more than 3 billion residents of the world. The poor of Asia, Africa, Latin America and tens of millions living inside the United States and Europe have seen little or no benefits from the much heralded economic model. Indeed, since George I proclaimed this 'new world order' in 1991, according to World Bank and UN figures, Third World unemployment and cases of preventable illness have risen while income and life expectancy have dropped. Compared with their counterparts in the 'hopeful years' of the 1960s, today's rich have much more and the very poor possess much less of the world's wealth.

Nor has so-called democracy substantially prevented 'democratic' armies from killing their own people in scores of Third World countries, or 'democratic' police from torturing and jailing those who vocally oppose the system.

I ask my wife, sort of whimsically:

'Will some reporter ever ask the Missionary in Chief, President George W. Bush, if he might want to take his democratic, free market export product back to the proverbial drawing board before demanding that the rest of the world buy it or else?'

'Wake up,' she replies. 'You're dreaming!'

ARGENTINA GOT IMF'D*

Ah, if only the proverbial fly on the wall in the executive offices of the IMF and World Bank had had a mini recorder and taped the conversations that ensued after Argentina, the most obedient Latin American follower of IMF orders, went belly up! One economist said in a huff on National Public Radio that the Argentine workers brought down the system. 'They think they deserve things like housing and transportation. You can't run a sound economy when people have those expectations.'

'Why are people rioting in Argentina?' my teenager asked. 'Do the International Monetary Fund, neo-liberalism and the US government relate to their situation?'

Well, I began, US government officials have acted as secular disciples for a system known as neo-liberalism, not to be confused with Jesse Jackson's liberal politics. The neo-liberal order pushes governments to seek foreign investment as their top priority. To make their country attractive to greedy, multinational entrepreneurs, governments then cut subsidies to the poor and spend less on social services. They devalue the currency so workers must spend more hours working. Say a loaf of bread used to cost $1. By devaluing the currency, the bread essentially doubles in price, meaning the worker has to toil twice as many hours to buy the same loaf. Governments also reduce import tariffs so foreign goods can enter the country without penalty, which hurts local manufacturing and helps large foreign exporters.

'I understand all that,' she said. 'But Argentina used to be such a rich country, full of educated people and advanced technology and great public services. What happened to all that wealth?'

Well, I replied, the government under President Carlos Menem (1989–1999) followed the IMF formula for attracting foreign investment. Under his Finance Minister, Domingo Cavallo, Argentina privatized public wealth. Needless to say, Menem got his cronies involved personally in these

---

* Originally appeared on *Pacifica Network News* and later in the *Anderson Valley Advertiser*, January 9, 2002 (substantially revised for the book). Together with the departure of major government officials (including President Fernando de la Rua and the Finance Minister, Domingo Cavallo) and massive rioting, a state of siege was called in Argentina on December 20, 2001.

privatization transactions. Hey, what are friends and family for? The Argentine press reported some of this hanky-panky. But the IMF officials shrugged their shoulders. Why should they get excited about corruption in the Third World?

'Where did the IMF idea originate?' she asked.

In 1944, US officials and leaders of the allied economic powers planned post-war reconstruction at Bretton Woods. They anticipated that Western European nations would need large loans to reconstruct their infrastructures and give them a kick start, but, with a highly skilled and disciplined workforce laboring under austerity wages, private capital would pour in to speed recovery. The pain felt by the European working class would not endure for long, they thought, and in the meantime the IMF's loan formula would provide crucial aid to balance of payment problems of countries whose treasuries had been emptied by the war. They didn't intend their formula to apply to Third World countries that lacked the skilled and disciplined workforce and developed infrastructure of Western Europe. And Western Europeans also had political systems with clear accountability provisions.

'Huh?' she said.

Take the Argentine government as an example of less than full accountability. The government sold public property like railroads, utilities, natural resources, roads, etc. to private companies, who then exploited them to the max, allowed some of them to deteriorate and then sold some of them back to the state for more than they paid. Obviously, bribes and payoffs took place. The state then resold some of the properties again and the cycle continues. This same formula worked to the detriment of the Mexican public when privatization took place there in the late 1980s and in the 1990s. Indeed, the same negative result has occurred in almost every other Third World country where the IMF imposed it.

'Give me some examples,' she demanded.

Mexico sold off some highways to private enterprise. The CEOs of the buying companies drained the bank accounts of their new companies and put the profits into their pockets. They didn't spend money to maintain the roads and then appealed to the government to help them fix the roads and keep them open. And, I added, they call all of this free market or free trade.

'Wow,' she said. 'Who designed such a system?'

The idea dates back to liberal—meaning no state interference in the economy—dreamers in the nineteenth century. These Utopians thought that free trade would solve the world's problems. Their economic dream never materialized of course. But since the 1960s, spurred by famous economists like the University of Chicago's Milton Friedman, IMF officials have revived and promoted this so-called free market model on the illusion that Third World countries could 'develop' and become like the United States, Japan and Europe.

After Pinochet and his uniformed thugs blew away the civilian government of Chile and imposed a military dictatorship in 1973, they invited the so-called Chicago School, led by Friedman's disciple Arnold Harberger, to try out their free market model in Chile. Irony? Impose a free market system on a totalitarian dictatorship? Well, without a constitution, political parties or debate, free press, trade unions or even a semblance of workers' rights, the model proved somewhat effective. That is, Chilean workers suffered a huge drop in income, worked harder than ever because they had to and the investors smiled at their profits. Seventeen years of military dictatorship under Pinochet might be the prerequisite for this 'free' model.

'But,' she concluded, 'looking at the other Third World countries who have tried the model, like Mexico and Argentina, development didn't exactly happen the way it was supposed to?'

Not in Argentina, nor practically anywhere else in the Third World, I said. You see, the IMF, first and foremost, sought to insure stability for foreign investors. So, IMF wise men advised Argentina to borrow, which it did. The Argentine government, like others in South America, then accumulated an un-payable debt, which it had to service at high interest rates. Indeed, the interest alone on Argentina's debt would bankrupt most Third World countries.

To make sure that investors wouldn't lose their money, the IMF advised Argentine leaders to peg their peso to the US dollar. But the peso was actually worth less than the dollar and, by pegging it to a higher valued currency, the IMF contributed to disaster. You see, by putting the peso on a false par with the dollar, you raise the price of imported goods and make Argentine exports expensive as well.

Also, corruption sucks away some vital funds. The point is that the IMF insisted that, instead of changing its model to something corresponding to Argentine reality, the Argentine poor had to bear more and more austerity for the model to work. So, the state cut benefits and subsidies to the working people and instead offered goodies to lure investors. Workers toiled harder for less under the promise that ultimately so much foreign capital would enter Argentina that all problems would be solved.

'So,' she said, 'workers sacrificed for an economic experiment that couldn't work—except for those who made big profits by speculating and having their bets secured?'

You got it, I said. So, as in many Third World countries where governments have imposed the IMF formula, workers in Argentina rioted and overthrew the government on December 20, 2001. Now, a new and very weak government has to decide: should it favor the propertied classes and let them take their money out of the bank in dollars, or help the working class that thinks it has won what we call entitlements, like social security benefits, health plans etc?

'What's gonna happen?'

I don't know. But Argentine events will not help advance Bush's Free Trade Area of the Americas hallucination and we'll probably see populist and maybe even fascist-like politics in Argentina. The Argentine left is demanding that the government respond to the needs of Argentine workers, not to the greed of the investors, who have already extracted hundreds of millions in profits from Argentina. The anti-IMF, anti-free trade riots continue. Remember, they occurred in Egypt, Venezuela, the Philippines and other places where the IMF, backed by the US government, imposed the very same formula. One thing is certain, the Argentine workers and middle class are mighty unhappy.

'I understand,' she said, 'they really got IMF'd.'

CHILE'S ULTRA-LITE SOCIALIST MODEL[*]

Free marketers hold up Chile as the one bright light in Latin America's otherwise dim picture. Few people, however, discuss the historical price Chileans have paid for the limited success of their government's economic policies. But I suppose amnesia is preferable to a frontal lobotomy.

In March 2000, I attended the inauguration of Ricardo Lagos, the first socialist president elected in Chile since the Chilean military deposed Salvador Allende in the bloody September 11, 1973 coup. General Pinochet had ruled for the 17 years which followed the coup. He murdered more than 3,000 of his political opponents and tortured and exiled tens of thousands. Then, in 1990, after Pinochet submitted to international pressure and allowed Chileans to vote, the public chose a coalition of Christian Democrats and socialists. They governed for a decade with the Christian Democrats claiming the presidency.

---

[*]   Originally appeared on *Pacifica Network News* and later in the *Anderson Valley Advertiser*, November 28, 2001 (substantially revised for the book). In mid November, I attended a human rights conference in Santiago, Chile.

Thirty years after Allende's historic 1970 victory, the socialists won again. Thousands of young people jumped in groups shouting 'Bring Pinochet to trial.' The ex-dictator had recently returned from 15 months of house arrest in England and Chile. A Spanish judge had charged Pinochet with crimes against humanity in 1998. The British House of Lords had upheld the jurisdiction of the Spanish court to try him. But a high-level deal between the British, Chilean and Spanish governments led to Pinochet's getting sprung on 'medical grounds.'

Chilean Judge Juan Guzman, emboldened by judicial rulings abroad stripping Pinochet of immunity, opened a case against him in Santiago for his role in disappearing hundreds of people. Many of those who had suffered torture or lost parents and loved ones at the hands of the dictator's secret police and armed forces felt optimistic. Under Lagos, they believed, the government would summon the energy and will to bring the *criminal en jefe* to trial.

In the ensuing months, however, Chileans grew disenchanted. Instead of helping bring Pinochet to trial, government officials created roadblocks on the road to justice. The relatives of the dead and the disappeared began to sneer at Lagos and his ruling groups: they had gotten little help from the socialist President they helped elect.

I visited with Hortensia Bussi de Allende, Salvador Allende's widow, and their daughter Isabel, now running for re-election as a socialist deputy. Both women cling to the old socialist principles, but they have become a minority in the party. Most of the 'modern' Chilean socialist officials, like their counterparts in Western Europe and other Third World countries, focus on the trendy issues, like getting Chile admitted into NAFTA and securing F-16 fighter jets from the Pentagon and Lockheed—so as to 'feel strong' and of course not offend Chile's air force.

In November, the US agreed to send the jets—without the missiles attached to them. President Lagos complained that this insulted Chilean sovereignty. Imagine, the US government didn't trust sending its missiles to Chilean generals, some of whom are accused of torturing fellow citizens during the Pinochet years! The Pentagon heavies didn't object to the torture, mind you. They feared flack from liberals in Congress if they were caught sending advanced weapons to torturers.

Before the 2001 congressional elections, polls indicated that the Chilean right would gain legislative seats. Unlike most of the urbane socialists who bragged about the performance of Chile's stock market, the rightist candidates campaigned in poor neighborhoods on populist issues. Although Chile has escaped the horrible fate of Argentina, whose foreign debt drowns its economy, you don't have to look hard for signs of poverty.

On the sidewalk outside of Santiago's pre-Columbian museum, several pre-Colombians begged for coins; others slept by the entrance, drunk, depressed or both. Sharing Santiago's crowded downtown streets with very shabbily dressed people, walked the trendy set, with cellphones glued to their ears, doing business—or at least pretending. When I asked some young people about the Pinochet years, or the Allende times, a glazed look froze their faces and they changed the subject. They love to discuss 'business' and all things American, however.

'It's important to have historical memory intact,' Mrs. Allende told me, 'to remember the noble democratic experiment we had undertaken.' Some day, it might be tried again—adapted of course to modern times.

LIES, TRUTH, TRIVIA AND TRANSCENDENT ISSUES IN MONTERREY*

The business elite and the professional economists don't seem to observe—or don't care about—the horrific results that ensue when political rulers dutifully apply their IMF model. Behind this model, economics and political power merge. In Monterrey, however, the test of obedience to both political and economic power revolved around the 'important' issue of image: Bush versus Castro.

'It happened in old Monterrey,' the nostalgic love song informs us. But unfortunately the mass media misinformed the public about the nature of the acrimonious events that occurred in this industrialized Mexican city during the week of March 18–22, 2002. Once again, the triteness of gossip generated by Washington's anti-Cuba politics intruded at a summit meeting designed to confront the world's leading economic issues.

Mexican President Vicente Fox, host of the UN International Conference on Financing for Development, had announced that he wanted to direct the delegates at the meeting to 'strengthen the policies and institutions required to mobilize domestic resources and attract foreign investment.' The developing countries, Fox said, had 'the primary responsibility ... to implement sound economic policies, strengthen the rule of law, create fair and impartial judicial systems, and fight impunity and corruption.'[52]

Having stated these noble goals, Fox vaguely challenged the 'industrialized nations in North America and Europe' to show 'they are genuinely committed to supporting the new drive for development by reversing the

---

* Originally appeared in *Progreso Weekly*, April 11, 2002.

persistent decline in official development assistance, by opening their borders to trade, and by reducing subsidies to agriculture.'[53]

Fox also noted that 'agricultural produce from developing countries often would be highly competitive and a source of desperately needed income if developed countries didn't impose artificial market barriers.'[54]

Ironically, Fox's Foreign Minister then proceeded to obey the very man who had just reimposed tariffs to protect US steel from market competition and had lavished US agribusiness with billions in subsidies to give them an edge over less subsidized Third World producers.

W, preaching the virtues of the free market while practicing the vice of protectionism, had placed a secret condition on his attendance in Monterrey. Mexico had to assure the White House that Bush would not share any space or time with Cuba's President Fidel Castro.

The White House apparently feared that even an accidental joint appearance with Cuba's President would ruin W's pristine reputation with extremist Cuban exile constituents who, you should recall, had donated oodles of money to the Republican candidate and helped intimidate Florida vote counters. These 'patriots' might not understand that presidential obligations could place George W. Bush at the same international meeting as the communist, atheist Devil himself.

So, as those who conspired to keep Fidel from the Monterrey meeting should have anticipated, Cuba's *jefe* turned a perceived slight from Fox into a 'newsworthy' event that embarrassed both the Mexican President and his Foreign Minister. As he concluded his speech with a blistering critique of those who ran the world economy, Fidel asked for the 'indulgence' of the heads of state 'since I will not be able to accompany you any longer.'[55]

Having gotten everyone's attention by announcing his unscheduled early departure from the conference, Castro further tantalized the audience by claiming that a 'special situation created by my participation in this Summit obligates me to immediately return to my country.'[56]

The press quickly learned from eager Cuban 'leakers' that this 'special situation' involved the perfidy of Jorge Castañeda. Since becoming Foreign Minister in 2000, Castañeda had made it his practice to kiss US butt—and then some. On February 27, 2002, Castañeda's ambiguous remarks in Miami about keeping the doors of the Mexican Embassy open to all Cubans led to anti-Castro elements crashing a bus into the Mexican Embassy in Havana, to the chagrin of Mexico's ambassador who had to cope with unruly Cubans and ultimately call the police to evict them.

In 2001 Castañeda blatantly served US political interests and violated Mexico's long-standing rule against helping the Americans openly in their anti-Castro crusade. Castañeda led a move to condemn Cuba for human rights abuses at the UN Human Rights Commission in Geneva. Not only did this provoke critics to ask about Castañeda's double standards, since Mexico was arguably a far more blatant human rights violator than Cuba, but also what did Castañeda hope to achieve? For all of his servility to US demands, the United States had not given Castañeda his quid pro quo: legalizing millions of 'illegal' Mexican immigrants. So, instead of learning his lesson, that butt kissing the United States gets you nothing more than a brown nose, Castañeda again played the obedient servant role in the Monterrey meeting.

Cuban officials claim that Castañeda breached both the norms of dignity and protocol when he informed them—prior to the meeting—that Bush would not attend the Monterrey session 'if Castro attended.' Castro claims that the United Nations—not Mexico—had invited him to participate in the Monterrey Summit. *Granma*, the official organ of Cuba's Communist Party, claimed that Castañeda, during his and Fox's visit to Cuba on February 3, 2002, had requested to other Cuban officials that 'Comrade Fidel be asked the favor of not attending the conference in Mexico,' but lacked the guts 'to raise the subject' to Fidel's face.[57]

However, the *Granma* editorial avers, only '24 hours before his departure for Monterrey' Mexican officials asked the Cuban President not to attend the Summit.

> After strenuous exchanges of opinion and with great difficulty the Mexican Government consented to an agreement accepted by Cuba— with no other alternative—that the head of our delegation would withdraw in the afternoon of the 21st. The Commander-in-Chief kept his word, but could not leave without giving a brief explanation, as much for the Cuban people as for international public opinion.[58]

Castañeda denies that he tried to limit Castro's participation. Yet, according to *Granma*, which claims to have ample evidence to back its claims, Castañeda 'shamefully lied about events he knew only too well.'[59]

As if to rub salt into the open wound caused by Castañeda's peculiar protocol practices, *Granma* absolved from blame President Fox 'at a time when serious human and economic problems are awaiting a solution on which depends the fate of millions of Mexicans who live illegally in lands snatched from their country.' Continuing with its barely disguised attack on the Mexican Foreign Minister who has done little to alleviate the plight of Mexican laborers in the United States, *Granma* claimed sympathy with the hundreds who 'die every year crossing and re-crossing borders ... and suffer discrimination and the violation of their most basic human rights.'[60]

Castro's premature departure put Castañeda in the hot seat. The Mexican media severely criticized him as did Mexico's Congress. More importantly, the incident skewed Bush's primary goals for his brief trip to Latin America. Instead of promoting his free trade with aid package, Bush had to respond to the question: Did he 'pressure' Castro? This issue took center stage, rather than his much publicized attempt to promote his new visage as friend of the poor and herald of the very economic model that Castro dismembered in his Monterrey speech.

More important than who said what to whom or the apparent breach of protocol, were the differences between the economic models represented by Castro and Bush at Monterrey. Reported in less than a paragraph by most of the prestige media, Fidel's critique of corporate globalization cut to the core of imposing issues that confront more than 3 billion of the world's 6 billion people.

The Cuban leader described Bush's model for trade and development, the current economic order, as 'a system of plundering and exploitation like no other in history.' What Castro called 'a huge casino,' Bush called a healthy way of doing business. What Bush called 'investment,' Castro labeled as 'speculative operations completely disconnected from the real economy.'[61]

In Bush's mental picture, the US-dominated economic order has served the people well. After all, the people he knows possess wealth. Indeed, most are millionaires many times over. Castro's vision, however, includes that part of the world that 'lives in underdevelopment, and extreme poverty.' Bush foresees his model as the instrument to close the economic gap. Castro claimed, presenting UN statistics to back up his argument, that the current system 'far from narrowing the gap' has widened it. 'The situation has reached such extremes,' declared Fidel, 'that the assets of the three wealthiest persons in the world amount to the GDP of the 48 poorest countries combined.'[62]

Citing UN figures, Castro said that 826 million were starving in 2001, 854 million adults were illiterate in 2002 'while 325 million children do not attend school.' Two billion people had no access to low cost medications. 2.4 billion lacked basic sanitation. 'No less than eleven million children under the age of five perish every year from preventable causes while half a million go blind for lack of vitamin A.'[63]

President Bush who, after his meeting with U2 rock star Bono, claimed he understood the need to increase aid to the poor, still maintains that only the western economic model can solve world poverty. Castro claims this model has led to a 30 years higher life span in the developed world than for those living in Sub-Saharan Africa.

Bush implicitly blames the poor for their own plight. They don't work hard enough—presumably as he has all his life—and they elect corrupt governments. He offers a little more aid, but attaches strings that ensure that no US money goes to 'support corruption.' The very recent Enron affair has apparently already faded into the realm of ancient history for Bush. Enron CEOs of course stole far more than the corrupt Third World countries could have skimmed from US aid programs over a decade.

Compare Bush's self-righteous sermonizing approach to Castro's. 'The poor countries should not be blamed for this tragedy,' declared Fidel. 'They neither conquered nor plundered entire continents for centuries; they did not establish colonialism, or re-establish slavery; and modern imperialism is not of their making. Actually, they have been its victims. Therefore, the main responsibility for financing their development lies with those states which, for obvious historical reasons, enjoy today the benefits of those atrocities.'

As Bush works with IMF and World Bank officials to try to figure out how to squeeze ever more out of impoverished Third World countries and force them to make usurious interest payments on old loans, Castro demands that the 'rich world should condone their foreign debt and grant them fresh soft credits to finance their development. The traditional offers of assistance, always scant and often ridiculous, are either inadequate or unfulfilled.'

Castro went on to cite the late economist James Tobin's suggestions 'to curtail the irrepressible flow of currency speculation' and replace 'awful institutions like the IMF' with UN agencies in order to 'supply direct development assistance with a democratic participation of all countries and without the need to sacrifice the independence and sovereignty of the peoples.'

Unfortunately, the Consensus draft signed by the Monterrey attendees reflected little of Castro's thinking. The world's visionless heads of state seem to share one desire: to govern, period, no matter what the agenda.

They preside, as Castro intoned, 'over a world in which ever more sophisticated weapons [are] piling up in the arsenals of the wealthiest and the mightiest [which] can kill the illiterate, the ill, the poor and the hungry but they cannot kill ignorance, illnesses, poverty or hunger.'

Just before he announced his departure Castro called for 'a farewell to arms.' People clapped. 'A better world is possible,' he concluded.[64]

Castro delivered the only prophetic speech at the meeting. Delegates cheered, then they went about their business of perpetuating the very order that has caused such intense suffering for the world's poor, devastated its environment and led to arguably the most dangerous arms build-up in world history. Yes, 'it happened in old Monterrey.'

VICENTE FOX DESERVES THE
FLAT TIRE OF THE YEAR AWARD*

After Castro's premature departure from the Monterrey conference, Vicente Fox continued to deny the Cuban leader's charges that Mexico had asked Castro to leave so that Bush would attend. Castro then assembled the media and played a tape of a phone conversation that he had secretly recorded. On it, the Mexican President clearly asks him to leave before Bush arrives. Fox deserved his Monterrey humiliation, not just for kissing Bush's ass, but for continuing to apply an economic model and insist on a growth plan that has not worked in his country or elsewhere. For his persistence, however, I gave him my special prize.

In 2000 the first freely elected President of Mexico promised his voters substantial economic growth through his free market plans, a rapid settlement of the Chiapas mess and a campaign to wipe out human rights abuse and corruption. Despite my skepticism, I felt optimistic. After all, by choosing Vicente Fox of the conservative National Action Party (PAN), Mexicans unseated the Institutionalized Revolutionary Party (PRI), which for 70 years had held a monopoly of state power and abused it to the max.

After one year, I conclude, however, that Fox deserves an award—the flat tire prize for failing to complete promises.

Instead of the 7 per cent economic growth rate he pledged, he has delivered 0 per cent. Yes, the US recession and the reverberations after the 9/11 events caused a reduction in orders for the maquiladoras. Needless to say, the post September 11 'security' measures increased the amount of delivery time for products that cross the Mexico–US border. Investors traditionally respond to recession by reducing their investment, but Fox's plan for Mexican prosperity depended on ever-lasting prosperity, which had not yet occurred in human history (see the great economist Joseph, in the Bible). And, as the saying goes, when the United States' economy sneezes, Mexico develops pneumonia. Over the last six months, to continue the metaphor, the United States has had a long-term running nose and hacking cough; Mexico has had a veritable epidemic of emphysema.

By basing Mexico's prosperity exclusively on foreign investment, Fox had tied Mexico's destiny to the capricious play of the speculators and the unpredictable ups and downs of the global economy. When recession hits and US and other foreign consumers cut back on their shopping habits, a former

---

*   Originally appeared on *Pacifica Network News* and later in the *Anderson Valley Advertiser*, January 2, 2002 (substantially revised for the book). I spent a week in Mexico in early December on a film shoot.

corporate executive—Fox was CEO of Coca-Cola in Mexico—ought to know that factory orders for goods fall off as well.

Now Mexico, which over the last decades has reversed its plans (1930–1960s) to achieve self-sufficiency in food staples, must buy massive amounts of US corn and beans to feed its people while it simultaneously suffers a serious reduction in national income.

In a moment of bravado in his campaign, Fox also boasted that he could make peace in Chiapas in 15 minutes. Some say he really meant 24 hours. A year after this piece of bragging, 50,000 Mexican troops still occupy the Mayans' land, stopping travelers on the jungle roads, occasionally arresting, raping and killing suspected Zapatista rebels. Poverty in Chiapas has become more aggravated.

Similarly, in indigenous-heavy Guerrero, troops stop travelers on the highway between the tourist meccas of Acapulco and Zihuatanejo, supposedly checking for arms and drugs. Military patrols in the Guerrero mountains hunt for guerrillas and members of the Peasant Ecologists Organization, who in the late 1990s had successfully stopped the Boise Cascade Corporation (located in Idaho and one of the world's largest timber corporations, Boise Cascade saw the opportunity for cheap labor and lumber in Mexico) from accomplishing the clear cutting of all their woodlands. The army, representing the political bosses who were making super-profits from the US-based multinational, arrested peasants—although the Constitution does not give them that power—tortured them, according to human rights monitors, and assassinated others. Indeed, army personnel are suspected of having assassinated earlier in 2001 Digna Ochoa,[65] a human rights lawyer who represented the peasant ecologists. Does Fox not control his army, as some Mexicans suspect? Was he just naïve? Or is he downright duplicitous?

In foreign policy, Fox appointed the clever, former leftist intellectual Jorge Castañeda, who ended all radical pretenses by announcing that principles would play no part in his foreign policy. A cab driver told me with a straight face, 'Fox and Castañeda together have set a Mexican record for kissing US ass. Not even when he was trying to get into NAFTA did former President Carlos Salinas behave as submissively with the gringos.'

'But,' he said, 'Fox has accomplished several important things. He's made it difficult for raped women to have abortions, for teenagers to wear mini skirts or for homosexuals to marry. Even more important,' he continued, 'our government has banned sexy brassiere ads and removed statues of Benito Juarez and erected new ones of the conquistadors, the guys who killed the Indians.'

'Oh,' he said, still without cracking a smile, 'Fox also allowed prices of medicine to rise beyond the reach of the poor, while he appropriated more money than any previous president for foreign travel—and he got married. So, don't say he hasn't done anything.'

But, I said, he was freely elected.

'Yes,' the driver admitted. 'Long live democracy. May it some day relate to human life in Mexico.'

A REPORT ON NAFTA AND THE STATE OF THE MAQUILAS*

In the last four decades, tens of millions of Mexicans have moved from the impoverished countryside to the cities, where they have found work in or around the maquilas, the foreign-owned factories that export parts or finished goods. This low wage and relatively productive workforce attracted foreign investment. In 1993, the US Congress formally endorsed NAFTA. Foreign investors received an extra incentive: they now had the equivalent of the US Government's Good Housekeeping Seal of Approval. Both President Clinton and now President Bush have claimed NAFTA to be a great success. I decided to make my own assessment.

After spending a few late June days in the El Paso–Juarez area, I can report that NAFTA works fabulously, if you're a speculator—I mean investor—or a multinational corporate CEO and your Juarez branch plant survived the US recession and 9/11 and remained open.

A few Mexican millionaires who lease land for industrial parks and those who feed off contracts to the export factories have also fared well. For the more than 1 million Mexicans working in the Juarez maquilas who have not lost their jobs recently, well, they've survived, which they could not have done had they remained on the unproductive land of their origin.

The contemporary maquilas represent yet another industrial revolution. Instead of reading about Manchester or Leeds in the 1840s, visit contemporary Tijuana or Juarez. Today's equivalent of a Dickensian saga centers around the maquila, which attracts country folk to cities for jobs and then leads them into human dramas.

People from tradition-bound communities have made the difficult transition to non-community life where each person must suspect rather than respect his neighbor—themes for modern *telenovelas*. In Juarez, for example, in the last eight years the remains of more than 250 women have

* Originally appeared in *Progreso Weekly*, July 4, 2002. Written in Juarez, Chihuahua, Mexico, while filming scenes for a forthcoming documentary *We Don't Play Golf Here*.

been found raped and mutilated. Almost all of them worked in maquilas. The police have 'caught the murderers' several times; yet the slaughter continues.

Ciudad Juarez, across the once mighty, but now trickling, Rio Grande River has grown cancerously. Yes, growth has little to do with development. Its barren, sandy hills have sprouted unplanned *colonias* (euphemism for hideous slums). Rural families arrive after surrendering to the fact that the land no longer supports them. They find jobs in the export factories, patch together homes from pieces of wood, metal and plastic, and find ways to tap into the power line (some get fried). They wait for the circulating water and gas trucks blasting 'La Cucaracha' on their speakers to bring the needed material for life and cooking. The families often store the drinking and washing water in old metal chemical barrels. The air, once just dusty during the high wind season, now reeks of emissions from factories and the stench of unmuffled auto and bus exhaust.

In *colonias* like Anapra and Lago Poniente, the rural folks rapidly acquire urban ways. They try to raise their kids to become academic achievers or send them into the maquilas in their mid teens to contribute to scarce family income. Alarming numbers of young people turn to drugs, prostitution and gang delinquency. The local government has not built parks or playgrounds.

The shacks in the *colonias* face unpaved, rocky streets where mangy dogs drop their loads and little kids run barefoot through the summer dust and excrement. Ana Maria, mother of three, and Catalina, mother of seven, agreed that for all the horrors of slummy urban life, at least Juarez meant certainty of employment. That was then, in 2000, when most of the maquilas boasted 'help wanted' signs and ran three shifts a day. Employment neared 100 per cent. An unhappy worker in Factory A could quit and find work at Factory B across the street where the wages were five centavos an hour more or which had better cafeteria food. That workplace mobility has ended with the onset of recession.

Take Ciudad Juarez, the birthplace of Mexico's maquilas. Less than a year ago, many of Juarez's more than 250 export factories ran three shifts a day. The city government claimed full employment. Now, Juarez suffers 17 per cent unemployment. Calculate the meaning of this 'official' figure in human terms. Most families need two or three maquila salaries just to survive!

Thanks to the growth of the maquilas, between 1965 and today Juarez has grown from a sleepy border town on the other side of the Rio Grande River from El Paso, Texas, into an industrial behemoth whose population may well have tipped the 2 million mark. Likewise, Tijuana, across the border from San Diego, California, has suffered a dramatic rise in unemployment.

Then recession developed in the United States, followed by the September 11, Al-Qaeda attacks. US recession meant maquila depression. Over the last

18 months, over 250,000 factory workers have lost their jobs in Mexico. Ironically, some of the very factories that moved from the United States in the 1980s and 1990s to take advantage of 'cheap Mexican labor,' now find compelling reasons to lower wages even further. They have begun to shift operations to Asia.

Catalina and Ana Maria, with their many children to support, have received pink slips. The once buzzing factories where they worked have transmogrified into misshapen tombstones; industrial parks have turned into industrial cemeteries. Creeping weeds and blowing plastic and paper litter now cover a once buzzing parking lot in front of Quality Industrial Services. A lone security guard shares the space with a scruffy cat and an elusive bird. 'It's difficult,' the guard told me, 'to see maquilas shutting down, moving to China, or wherever.' He blamed last year's US economic downturn for putting Mexicans out of work. 'But, that's the way it goes,' he concluded with a sigh.[66]

On the surface, says Chihuahua sociologist Victor Quintana, 'the job losses come from the US recession and the post-9/11 shocks, but in reality that's a smoke screen for deeper causes.' The maquila model, Quintana predicts, has exhausted its potential. Mexico cannot compete with China.

The maquilas still account for about half of Mexico's almost 150 billion annual exports. But efficient as Mexican laborers have proven themselves in global competition, they cannot match Chinese workers for the low wage labor championship. Quintana sees maquilas eroding rapidly.

'But,' Quintana says, 'the model has done its damage.' 'Two years ago,' he continues, 'Chihuahua led Mexico in high employment; today, Chihuahua leads in unemployment.' Thanks to lay-offs from factory shutdowns or factories moving or reduction of shift, Chihuahua has lost more than 100,000 jobs.

According to a June 20, 2002 *Washington Post* story, over the last two years more than 500 foreign-owned assembly-line factories in Mexico moved to China. The company accountants concluded that the wage differential between the two Third World countries more than covers the increased costs of shipping and the inconveniences of distance. In a Juarez-run maquila, where the cost of living runs at about 75 per cent that of El Paso across the river, a newly employed machine operator earns just under $8 a day, whereas his counterpart in China makes only a quarter of that pathetic wage.

Quintana doesn't mourn what he believes is the end of the maquila era. He thinks that NAFTA and the whole free trade model launched the equivalent of a cultural offensive against the majority of the world's poor. Quintana insists that the maquila represents far more than a new form of production. 'It dictates how we relate, how we live, what we do, consume.

It dictates individualism, destroys community. It's a form of terrorism, which leads people to ways of avoiding life; booze, crack and cult religions. It inundates us with its cultural propaganda.'

The maquila, asserts Quintana, has its own discourse, 'one that mocks traditional values like cooperation and solidarity. Its only values are individualism and competition.' Quintana has little patience with the rich and powerful, like President Vicente Fox himself, who wring their hands over 'losing our traditional values while they eagerly bring the value-destroying maquilas into the country for economic growth.'

Maquilas offer growth in productivity rates, but also in destruction. 'Those who preach that we should respect Nature invite the maquilas in who destroy Nature. Maquilas destroy people and their natural bonding. Maquilas are beyond cruel. They embody the impersonality of multinational corporate capitalism.'

Leticia Ortiz exemplifies Quintana's point. She came to Juarez from the countryside 19 years ago and worked her way up in a large maquila to become head of personnel. Then, without warning, she received her unceremonious dismissal. The CEOs located in some First World city had decided to capitalize on rock-bottom Chinese wages and move their plants to China, where productivity was just as high. Bitter?

'No, just disappointed,' she said. 'After working my way up for all those years I guess I foolishly developed a sense of loyalty to the company, a sense that was not reciprocated. They didn't even pay me what they owed me for severance according to the law. But it would take too long and it would be too expensive to fight it, so I accepted their less than generous offer.'

After receiving her pink slip, Leticia said she went home and cried for hours. Then, she said, 'I basically slept for the next six months. I guess you could call it depression.'

Juarez opened its first maquilas in 1965 in order to deal with a recently laid off labor force of hundreds of thousands of migrant workers who could no longer work in the Texas cotton fields thanks to a newly designed machine that replaced them.

US investors gradually learned of the lucrative possibilities for investment on Mexico's northern border. Low wages and a productive workforce, low taxes and no environmental regulation or costs related to agencies such as OSHA (Occupational Safety and Health Administration) made Mexico attractive. But, gradually, independent unions, backed by some AFL–CIO unions, began to move into the border cities and their appearance—plus rising cost of living—produced a rising impact on wages.

Nevertheless, until 2001, investment in Mexican maquilas had continued to rise. In 1993, NAFTA provided the kosher stamp for wary investors and the rate of maquila growth had reached double digits. It provided further tax-free incentives for maquila owners and facilitated plans for efficient corporate integration.

US companies ship raw materials to Mexico and then import finished parts or assembled products tax-free: electronics, electrical goods, automobiles and trucks and trailers or their parts, wood and plastic products and textiles.

When the 1965 maquila experiment began, Juarez attracted only a handful of factories. Now, almost 4,000 of these mostly foreign-owned export production plants dot the landscapes of border cities like Juarez, Tijuana, Mexicali, Nogales, Matamoros. Maquilas have also moved into the interior of the country.

Some Juarez plant owners, anticipating labor problems, built automated, even robotized factories to keep the labor force at a minimum. An Italian-owned factory manufactures TV and computer cases made in a mold and extracted by a robot. The plant uses comparatively few workers. Pasquale Galizzi, the Italian plant manager, said it made strategic sense to open a plant in Juarez, given its proximity to the US border. 'The wages we pay here are about one fourth of what we would have to pay in Milan,' he added.

What happens now that some of these people have become unemployed? According to Quintana, a few return to the villages and live in squalor. Some still try to traverse the difficult obstacles of the US border. Near El Paso, however, since the 9/11 attacks, almost no one tries successfully to cross.

Further west, in the hottest and remotest sections of the Arizona desert, where summer temperatures top 115 degrees, the coyotes lead their human prey. These dealers in human flesh offer their crossing-the-border services for a price to those desperately wanting to reach US territory. The coyotes assure their clients of plentiful water. However, the coyotes often abandon their charges just at the point when the water runs out and the temperature becomes inhospitable for human life. Through mid June 2002 alone, more than 20 Mexicans, including an eleven-year-old girl, had died trying this route. Regularly, stories appear in the media about speeding vans carrying undocumented workers crashing and killing the occupants in attempts to elude border patrol chasers.

Since October 2002 almost 50 Mexicans have fallen trying to make it to the Tucson area. US immigration laws are death laws, said one Mexican border resident. Thanks to the newly militarized border patrol vigilance the traditional flow of Mexicans into the United States has noticeably decreased.

The usual zones have too many patrols, so the perilous desert has become the choice of the truly desperate and adventurous.[67]

As a result of this crackdown on *braceros* or *mojados* most of the newly unemployed will remain in Juarez. 'The population here may have reached 3 million,' speculates Juarez environmentalist Felix Perez. No one has counted. Each day 'hundreds, maybe thousands, arrive at the bus station, looking for work in the maquilas.'

'I'm staying in Juarez,' Ana Maria said. 'It's rough here, but it's impossible where I came from.'

Maquila missionaries still promise potential investors that Mexico's workforce can compete for low wages and high productivity with other Third World countries. That's global competition! Which country can offer its people for the lowest wages, can promise polluting industries the least environmental regulation, the lowest taxes, the least workplace monitoring for health and safety and the least prospect for unionization! This is the free market. This is democracy!

To keep it healthy, if you listen to President Bush or President Fox, we need more of the same. President Bush makes no reference to the labor, environmental and social horrors that have developed alongside what has become known euphemistically as 'free trade.' Indeed, he pushes hard and patriotically to expand his free trade authority, called fast track, because Congress will not have a chance to debate the details.

A few days in Juarez should enlighten any sensitive person to the fact that there is no guiding brain in this maquila process. The bottom line, which dictates corporate policies, dictates all of life.

THE ENVIRONMENT AND THE MAQUILAS*

After spending a period of weeks investigating labor and environmental conditions on the US–Mexico border, I have concluded that although the production system used to inundate us with commodities—globalization—lacks a human brain, it has an excellent calculator. The managers of the multinational factories and the developers of the giant industrial parks on the border cities on the Mexican side possess advanced university degrees and speak coherently about bottom lines. But I find no evidence of a sensible intelligence. These high IQ human specimens with MBAs from prestigious universities represent a production, distribution and sales system that

---

* Originally appeared in *Progreso Weekly*, July 18, 2002. Written after watching supervised workers in a foreign-owned factory in Juarez dumping toxic waste into a canal.

accumulates wealth, raw and human materials. They live under the international laws of acronyms: NAFTA, GATT, WTO, the ubiquitous letters that mean free trade, neo-liberalism, globalization and of course the free market.

This global system runs on a rational basis, meaning it possesses measures to evaluate efficiency, but lacks human reason. For example, the system needs adequate resources, good water, air and land to continue to make the products it pushes relentlessly on all prospective buyers. Yet in order to make these commodities competitively it systematically ruins the earth's water, air and soil and destroys prematurely the essence of the very people who must work in its factories. In short, it defies the wisdom of the old Arab saying: don't shit in the plate you eat from.

Ciudad Juarez provides a dramatic illustration. In late June 2002 I stood on the south bank of a 20-foot-wide canal with sewer water (*aguas negras*) running through it. Osvaldo Aguinaba, an elderly farmer, stood on the other side. I tried not to let the stench rising from the rapidly moving stream interfere with my own stream of thought.

'So,' I shout across the fetid tributary, 'has this stinky water always run through here?'

'Yes, but it used to be pure sewage, you know, from human beings,' replies Osvaldo, dressed in white work clothes. He nodded his head and pointed at the putrid watercourse. 'But now it's mixed with the chemical wastes from the factories. Yes, those factories make most of this crap. It's ruining the countryside.'

Another elderly farmer in blue jeans, a red shirt and a baseball hat joined the one in white. He shook his head sadly. 'The government is allowing agriculture to die,' he said, pointing at the *aguas negras*.

From the farmers' side of the canal, standing on a ladder, one can see Texas, about half a mile away. On the Mexico side of the border, some 25 miles southeast of Juarez, alfalfa, sorghum and other cattle feed grow alongside cotton. 'They don't let us use the water to irrigate the fruit trees anymore,' the elderly farmer told me regretfully. ('Thank God,' I muttered to myself. But I wondered how much enforcement exists in rural Chihuahua.)

Osvaldo claimed that he still grew some wheat. I shuddered. 'Yes, the *aguas negras* drain into the fields. What can we do? There's been a long draught here. We have to eat. The animals have to eat. We have to grow our crops and sell them with whatever water we can find.'

People presumably eat the wheat and the meat and milk from the cows after they eat grains irrigated with this toxic river. A few miles further south a plant converts the solid waste into sludge bars, which it sells to farmers who then throw it onto their fields for fertilizer. I'm no scientist, but my nose tells me to move far away from the *aguas negras* and not consume anything that has had contact with them.

'The worst contaminators are the dangerous metals used in metal processing,' says Federico de la Vega, who studied Chemical Engineering at MIT and went home to Juarez to run a beer and soda pop distribution business and lease industrial parks to foreign maquilas. 'Cleaning metals for locks and other industrial products involves the use of chlorine, bromine and other truly toxic elements and I know that some of the maquila managers don't dispose of these poisonous residues properly. I worry especially about the health of pregnant women who come into contact with these dangerous compounds.'

Even Jaime Bermudez, the father and foremost promoter of Juarez industrial parks, admitted that environmental problems are serious. 'But these are problems we can solve,' he insists. 'The maquilas bring jobs and without jobs we have nothing.'

It reminded me of the mantra of some US labor unions some decades ago when their members demanded they confront chemical, nuclear and other workplace hazards. What's more important, a little crap in the air and water or a chance to earn a good living for your family? Be a tough working man. Environmental concerns are for sissies.

In border cities like Juarez, pollution hits one in the eyes, ears, nose, throat and lungs. 'First, we have the ancient busses,' says Felix Perez, a local environmental activist. 'These very used vehicles are the city's basic means of transportation. Not only are they extremely uncomfortable, they emit immense amounts of noxious exhaust.'

Perez points to the old US school busses which load workers going to and from the *colonias* where they live and the factories where they work. Some busses have little or no shock absorbers or springs as they bounce along the rutted, unpaved streets, lined with ramshackle huts, the housing for some of those who produce home furnishings, parts for fancy trailers and new auto and computer accessories. An average ride from *colonia* to factory takes almost an hour.

'The fact is,' Perez says, 'that we have no environmentally good transportation system. Add to that the contamination produced by the post-9/11 security measures taken by the US border agencies and you have truly non-breathable air.'

Perez refers to the extra time now required to cross the three bridges that link Juarez to El Paso, Texas. The delay has at least doubled the waiting time, so that Juarez and El Paso residents suck twice the emissions from the idling autos and trucks as they wait their turn to get cleared for entry by US customs. Needless to say, the Mexican vehicles have not passed emission control inspection.

Then there's the scarce water issue, Perez continues. The once mighty Rio Grande has been reduced to a trickle in parts of Juarez and what is left defies human contact. Juarez has five years of water remaining, he warns. For the future, the city officials have found a water source in the desert some miles from here, but it's located in a nuclear graveyard, where they buried among other things radioactive cobalt. So it may well have leaked into the water.

No one knew for sure whether the water would be safe to drink. But industrial planning in Third World countries doesn't take into account the human health factor. The rich will of course buy bottled water and Mexican officials assure investors that the supply of cheap labor in places like Mexico will remain abundant for decades to come. Indeed, companies tend to lay off older workers in favor of teenagers, most of whose health and energy will prove sufficient for production needs over the next five years. Workers in their forties show the marked increase of cancers, lung diseases and the syndromes associated with repetitive motion emerge.

Just as I left Juarez, in July 2002, Scientific-Atlanta, the second-largest US maker of television set-top boxes, announced that it had eliminated 1,300 jobs in Mexico because of declining demand. It had moved its manufacturing operations from Atlanta to Juarez in July 2001 and already had had to downsize. A company spokesman, Paul Sims, warned that more job cuts lay ahead.

So the new residents of Juarez who came there to make a living after the countryside economy dried up now face unemployment without any safety net and a physical environment that appears unsustainable. Why, I ask rhetorically, couldn't the brilliant people who developed the idea of maquilas as an economic base have thought about some worst-case scenarios? Or is it the very nature of the new world order, a global corporatism that dictates short-run boom and long-term disaster?

BREEDING CROWS*

If the blowback from US-dictated economic policies has produced misery, the repercussions of US imposed 'security' plans have led to a human rights nightmare.

In 1978, the FBI special agent Robert Scherrer explained to John Dinges and me (see *Assassination on Embassy Row*, our 1980 investigative work on the Letelier–Moffitt assassinations) about how he first learned of Operation

---

*   Originally appeared on *Pacifica Network News* and later in *The Lakewood Clarion*, December 7, 2000 (substantially revised for the book). Lakewood is a small town in New Jersey. On November 13, 2000, the US government declassified thousands of documents related to its behavior in Chile before and after the 1973 coup. These documents provided me with the familiar shock of recognition.

Condor. The Bureau had stationed Scherrer in the Southern Cone since 1972 where he served as Legal Attaché in the US Embassy in Buenos Aires. After receiving the FBI's urgent September 21, 1976 telex regarding the assassination that day of Orlando Letelier in Washington DC, he contacted an intelligence source whom he described as 'some Nazi Colonel in Military Intelligence' and from him he learned that the Letelier hit was the result of 'a wild Condor operation.'[68]

As Scherrer told us the story, documented in his September 28 cable to FBI headquarters, he thought he had struck intelligence pay dirt. 'Condor,' he wrote the Bureau in a top-secret report,

> Is the code name for the collection, exchange and storage of intelligence data concerning leftists, communists and Marxists recently established between the cooperating services in South America in order to eliminate Marxist terrorists and their activities in the area. In addition, Operation Condor provides for joint operations against terrorist targets in member countries. … Chile is the center of Condor, and in addition it includes Argentina, Bolivia, Paraguay and Uruguay. Brazil has also tentatively agreed to supply input for Operation Condor.[69]

Scherrer went on to describe 'a third and more secret phase of "Operation Condor,"' in which hit teams 'travel anywhere in the world … to carry out sanctions [including] assassinations, against terrorists or supporters of terrorist organizations from Operation Condor member countries.'[70]

Scherrer suggested that Condor operatives might well have assassinated Letelier. He was right. Within months of the assassination, the FBI discovered that Chile's secret police and intelligence chief, Colonel Manuel Contreras, had ordered the Letelier hit team to obtain false Paraguayan passports and recruit anti-Castro Cubans to actually do the button pushing on the bomb. The Condor method, Scherrer described, provided for the false passports and the 'local' hit men as means to cover the trail of the assassination planners. As Scherrer later told us, Condor carried out hundreds of assassinations, mostly in Latin America, but some in Europe as well. Scherrer helped crack the Letelier case for the FBI, presenting himself to us as an honest cop confronting murderous and dishonest members of his police profession abroad.

After he died, a decade ago, documents declassified in 2002 revealed that Scherrer had known about Condor more than a year earlier and, indeed, had participated in at least one of its operations, helping to hand over a leftist Chilean exile to Pinochet's secret police who then 'disappeared' the man.

I experienced the shock of recognition as I read about Scherrer's and the US government's knowledge and participation in Operation Condor before the Letelier assassination. By the summer of 1976, Condor had gotten 'out of control,' so the State Department requested that US ambassadors warn the heads of state of Condor countries to stop murdering so indiscriminately.

In July 1976, the Assistant Secretary of State for Inter-American Affairs, Harry Schlaudeman, cabled the US Ambassador to Chile, David Popper, to ask Pinochet to stop murdering his opponents abroad. Presumably, he could kill all he wanted inside Chile. Popper, a cable shows, argued that Pinochet, a world-class mass murderer, would take as an insult an inference that he was ordering murders.

Had Popper warned Pinochet, the Chilean dictator might well have taken umbrage, but that wouldn't necessarily have stopped him. He was determined to kill Letelier. And US authorities may have abetted him. In July 1976, the US Ambassador to Paraguay granted two Chilean secret police killers US visas. To cover his ass, he notified both Kissinger and George Bush, the CIA Director, and asked for confirmation of his action. They did not reply to his urgent cable. A week later, he revoked the visas when he grew nervous.

The CIA Director, Bush, received cable traffic about these two agents visiting the CIA, but neither he nor any other high official told the FBI or Orlando Letelier, the obvious target, that this might very well indicate that Pinochet planned to hit him. (On September 21, 1976, the assassins detonated a bomb they had placed under Letelier's car, killing him and Ronni Moffitt, a colleague at the Institute for Policy Studies where they both worked.)

Now, some 24 years after Pinochet's secret police thugs struck, the Justice Department still discusses indicting him—using information they've had for all these years but never used. The men who had created a crow in the person of Generalissimo Pinochet had not heard of the Spanish adage: 'Breed a crow and he'll pluck out your eyes.'

But in this case the trainers themselves were presidential crows.

The CIA followed orders from the White House. The chief crows showed little interest in listening to those who recited 'worst-case scenarios.' Indeed, even after 9/11, with the bin Laden blowback lesson dramatically before them, the CIA continues to provide sophisticated weapons to fanatic 'freedom fighters' who might temporarily serve US interests.

LESSONS FROM THE BAY OF PIGS*

In 1960, the CIA had recruited some of the Letelier killers as 'freedom fighters' to overthrow Fidel Castro. But those who orchestrated US policy then did not think about what damage would ensue to the United States from their impulsive actions.

What have US policymakers learned from what historian Arthur Schlesinger Jr. dubbed 'the perfect failure?' Schlesinger, who served as White House historian and high-level adviser to President John F. Kennedy, opposed the CIA-backed invasion of Cuba's Bay of Pigs by a brigade of some 1,500 anti-Castro Cuban exiles. But at the March 22–24, 2001 Bay of Pigs conference in Havana, Schlesinger said he had no apologies for his having written an official and obfuscating White Paper to justify that invasion of Cuba. 'It was too interesting to turn down an opportunity' to see how history was made from the inside, he said.

In mid April 1961, Schlesinger, who had achieved well-deserved praise for his scholarship on biographies of presidents Andrew Jackson and Franklin Roosevelt—and later for his opus on John F. Kennedy—had accepted the onerous task of speaking for the 'provisional government of Cuba,' which the CIA had invented and whose members it then brought to a small hut in the Everglades, presumably to hold there for shipment to Cuba after the invading brigade established its beachhead.

As Schlesinger and Adolph Berle, his White House partner in this undertaking, and also Chairman of the Board of the American Sugar Company that Castro had recently expropriated, told the media what policies and values the new US-backed government would uphold, TV listeners could hear cries in Spanish from the members of that 'government' inside the hut: 'Let us out. Let us out.' Schlesinger and Berle, embarrassed, nevertheless continued to speak for the members of this supposedly legitimate authority, whom the CIA had locked inside the hut because the Agency feared what they might say about Kennedy 'betraying the invasion.' Kennedy had refused to supply the CIA's army with US air support.

C. Wright Mills, the great sociologist, watched the scene on TV, pointed to Berle and Schlesinger and commented: 'They are examples of moral schlemiels.'[71]

---

* Originally appeared on *Pacifica Network News* and later in the *Anderson Valley Advertiser*, April 4, 2001 (substantially revised for the book). I attended the 40th Anniversary of the Bay of Pigs Conference held in Havana, Cuba, on March 22–24, 2001.

Unfortunately, Schlesinger didn't reflect on what moral lessons he learned from his Kennedy White House experiences. What did it mean, for example, that as a US official he conspired with others to overthrow a government in violation of US laws and treaties, albeit under the sacred aegis of anti-communism?

When Schlesinger repeated his phrase, 'a perfect failure' at the Bay of Pigs Conference, Cuban President Fidel Castro asked: 'But suppose the Bay of Pigs invasion had succeeded: would that not have led to an even greater US disaster?' Had President Kennedy called in US air power and then, presumably, marines to support the CIA's Cubans, the world might well have witnessed a Vietnam-style war 90 miles from US shores.

After Castro's army had defeated the invaders in 72 hours, President Kennedy accepted the blame, publicly. 'Victory has a thousand fathers,' he said on April 21, 1961, 'and defeat is an orphan.' But in private, instead of attempting to reach a *modus vivendi* with the Cuban revolutionary leaders, Kennedy appointed his brother, Robert Kennedy, the Attorney General, to avenge the 'fiasco' by directing the CIA to launch a campaign of terrorism.

In the post-Bay of Pigs era, Bobby Kennedy supervised Operation Mongoose, a plan to assassinate Castro and other Cuban leaders and to sabotage the Cuban economy through terrorism. Sam Halpern and Robert Reynolds, CIA officials who helped direct these operations, attended the 2001 Bay of Pigs seminar. They described these operations as 'stupid' and 'ineffective.' But Cuban government officials, some now retired, described how Cubans felt devastatingly punished by these violent raids. The damage to Cuba had reached the point in August 1961 whereby Castro put out the olive branch.

At the seminar, Richard Goodwin, a top White House adviser in 1961, described how he met Che Guevara in Montevideo, Uruguay. Goodwin said that he listened attentively as Che, speaking for the Cuban government, offered concessions: to pull back from the Soviet Union and especially from its military reach; to repay expropriated US companies for the property the Cuban government had confiscated; and, finally, to discontinue Cuba's hyperactive support for revolution in Latin America. In return, Che asked that the Kennedys desist from their assassination and terror campaign against Cuban officials and property.

The Kennedys rejected the détente offering and instead 'turned up the heat.' As it has now become known, the White House's terrorist campaign against Cuba throughout 1961 and into 1962 became an important factor in Castro's decision to accept Soviet ballistic missiles—which led to the terrifying Missile Crisis of October 1962. So, the Bay of Pigs and its aftermath, the Missile Crisis, in which the entire world fearfully awaited the outcome, derived from a US government decision: to break its own laws and the world's accepted morality so as to punish a disobedient regime in 'its sphere.'

What has Washington learned since then? Just as the Kennedy brothers didn't consider consequences, a 'worst-case scenario,' so too does the current Bush team eschew logical policy t█████ng. They do not consider, apparently, how difficult it will become█████ch an understanding in a post-Castro Cuba when Fidel no longer commands consensus. Indeed, the Bush administration has already employed a harder line—but without considering the consequences.

At the Havana meeting, five former members of the invading 1961 Cuban exile brigade extended their hands to their former mortal enemies. It only took a few seconds, but it held profound meaning. Why am I not holding my breath for the Bush gang to take a similarly sensible step toward the Cuban government?

US DOUBLE STANDARDS ON TERRORISTS*

The Al-Qaeda fanatics expressed their hatred for the American system by destroying the Twin Towers and a piece of the Pentagon. Over 44 years, the CIA aided and abetted anti-Castro fanatics to bomb, commit arson and assassinations in Cuba and, later, on US soil as well.

Fidel Castro's 'crimes' included his nationalizing US companies, engaging with the Soviet enemy and trying to export revolution. The United States did not try to negotiate or take Cuba to the International Court of Justice. Instead, the US government sought illegal means of 'retribution.' As children, Americans still memorize the first lines of the Declaration of Independence, the world's best argument for revolution. But the US government has long since dropped support for its contents.

When, in the course of their human events, Cubans made their 1959 revolution, the US reacted by sponsoring a terrorist counter-revolution. Given its current state of alert over airplane security, it would do well to recall that the US government eagerly permitted Castro-hating pilots to use US territory to fly into Cuba to actually drop leaflets and conceivably more dangerous objects (imagine the US response if anti-Americans based in

---

*   Originally appeared in *Progreso Weekly*, January 3, 2002. US troops in Afghanistan captured hundreds of men whom they characterized as terrorists and subsequently relabeled as 'enemy combatants.' I noticed that the word 'terrorist' did not apply to all terrorists. Indeed, the equation seemed to be: Muslim Terrorists = Cowards, Anti-Castro Cubans = Patriots.

Cuba—or anywhere else—should try to fly their planes over south Florida to drop leaflets!).

In late February 1996, Cuban MiGs shot down two propeller-driven planes, with four crew members, for 'invading Cuban air space.' The dramatic and deadly incident brought to world attention the fact that the United States had permitted pilots to over-fly Cuban airspace from Florida as if the Cuban government had grown so weak that anti-Castro forces could with impunity employ harassing tactics.

By 1990, most of the anti-Castro club in south Florida predicted that the Cuban government would soon fade. After all, the Soviet Union had imploded, leading to a nose dive by Cuba's dependent economy.

But despite the hardship resulting from the loss of Soviet aid and trade, the Castro regime remained. It no longer delivered cradle-to-grave security on which Cubans had counted. As internal complaints grew, alongside severe shortages, Castro did not have to face a strong political opposition on the island, because for three decades the United States had eagerly welcomed his opponents. Instead of causing trouble for the communist government on the island, a well-organized sector of the anti-Castro gang captured US–Cuba policy, and put it into the service of their narrow cause.

So, it did not surprise most Cuba observers when the US government encouraged Brothers to the Rescue to over-fly Cuba. The Brothers, forming in 1991 as a response to the Rafter Crisis, sent volunteer pilots, supposedly to spot rafters in the dangerous water separating Cuba and the Florida keys. The pilots would then radio their positions to nearby ships that would rescue them and bring them to Florida.

The Crisis arose when tens of thousands of Cubans, lacking jobs and sufficient food, propelled themselves toward Florida in inner tubes. Cuba charged that rather than engaging in humanitarian flights, however, the Brothers' real mission was to alert drug-laden ships in the Caribbean to the location of US coastguard vessels.

By 1995, when the size of Cuban migration—estimated at over 100,000 between 1991 and 1994—loomed as a serious political hazard, Washington and Havana signed a Migration Accord. The wave of rafters quickly subsided. And the Brothers changed their mission from alleged humanitarian rescue of rafters to outright confrontation.

In the spring of 1995, Jose Basulto, founder and leader of Brothers to the Rescue, filed a false flight plan, claiming a mission to the Bahamas, and instead flew his plane from Florida to Cuba and dropped anti-Castro leaflets over Cuban territory. On July 13, 1995, he returned to drop religious medals on populated areas, objects that could have hit people on the ground. How would the US air force have reacted to such shenanigans!

These flights coincided with a parallel campaign by militant anti-Castro exiles to cripple Cuba's tourist economy, her largest foreign exchange earner. The most notoriously violent anti-Castro emb Luis Posada Carriles, told reporter Ann Louise Bardach in a July 12–13, to 98 New York Times interview that executives of the prestigious Cuban American National Foundation had financed his scheme to shoot and plant bombs at tourist sites. One explosive killed an Italian tourist at a Havana hotel.

The FBI did not respond to Cuba's request to investigate the Florida-based exiles' role in the tourist bombings; nor did US authorities expend much energy looking into other terrorist actions emanating from south Florida. Clinton national security bureaucrats did plead with the Brothers to stop their over-flights and warned them that Cuban fighters could shoot them down.

In January 1996, one National Security Council official even wrote a letter on White House stationary to the FAA Commissioner requesting the suspension of the Brothers' licenses for having filed false flight plans. But the FAA, like the FBI, did not follow up. Nor did the White House! The FBI, instead of monitoring the activities of the US-based terrorists, targeted the Cuban spies, or so-called Wasp network, whose mission was to thwart terrorism.

In mid January, after getting little satisfaction from its formal demands that the State Department stop the over-flights, Cuba threatened 'grave consequences' for the next over-flight. Castro had already concluded that the US government would not protect Cuba from Florida-based terrorism. So, covertly, Cuba had infiltrated spies into south Florida. Posing as Castro-haters, the spies penetrated not US government agencies, to gather information, but some of the violent anti-Castro groups for the purpose of thwarting their terrorist activities. Cuba's intelligence chiefs considered Brothers to the Rescue as one of the most serious threats to island security. So, they directed some of the spies who were also pilots to infiltrate the Brothers' operations.

On February 24, 1996, when a trio of aircraft headed for Cuba with Brothers' boss Jose Basulto flying the lead plane, Cuban intelligence knew from several sources of the planned over-flight; not only their spies but from a US government official as well. On the night before the fatal flights, at a Washington DC concert, Richard Nuccio, the White House's Cuba point man, had informed two reporters that he knew of a planned over-flight the next day. Both of the reporters then called a Cuban official in Washington to get his reaction. So, a US official had indirectly informed the Cuban government of the Brothers' flight plan, a fact that the prosecutors downplayed or ignored when they later charged some of the spies with complicity in murder.

On that same February day, after receiving warnings from the US government not to fly over Cuban air space and direct orders from Cuban air control not to enter its territory, Basulto and his two partner airplanes entered Cuban air space. Cuban MiGs took off and shot down two of the three encroaching planes. Ironically, Basulto's plane escaped the missile attacks. (A debate continues as to whether the actual shoot-downs occurred over Cuban or international air space.)

The downing of the planes not only killed four people and set back US–Cuba relations, but it led also to the trial of the five spies. Seen in light of the September 11 acts, however, some of the government's witnesses who testified against the five men appear as anti-Castro equivalents of Al-Qaeda terrorists.

Take Basulto himself. In 1960–61, the CIA had trained this young man in the arts of violence, preparing him and thousands of others to invade Cuba at the Bay of Pigs. In August 1962, a year and a half after the Bay of Pigs fiasco, Basulto went on a CIA-authorized raid into Cuba during which he shot at a hotel, fired into a theater, and blasted a Havana residential section. Some 20 people died. He continued his violent anti-Castro adventures for some years after.

At the trial of the spies, Basulto testified that he had changed the violent approach of his youth to that of Gandhi and Martin Luther King, except, of course, in the case of Cuba where, he maintained, violence remained as a necessary tactic.

The south Florida jury that condemned the 'spies' evidently did not take history into account, beginning with those days before and during the April 1961 Bay of Pigs invasion, when the CIA concocted an air force that bombed and strafed Cuban targets; nor did they envision the thousands of other US-sponsored violent occasions when Cuban victims died, family members mourned, small children lost parents.

Indeed, on those rare occasions when the US government has brought cases to court for terrorist acts committed by anti-Castro Cubans, often with eyewitnesses testifying to the violence, south Florida juries have almost always acquitted the defendants. (Perhaps, given that the south Florida-based terrorists had acted with impunity over decades and those who have spoken against them have received threats—or worse—the jury members might have felt intimidated?)

In pre-September 11 times, Washington had consistently scoffed at Cuba's grievances. In the immediate post-Bay of Pigs era (January–April 15, 1961), for example, Cuba complained of more than 75 over-flights of its territory by US-based planes. 'Do unto others,' Washington officials might have said, 'what others cannot do unto you.'

But how would the United States react if unauthorized planes entered its air space? Ironically, in the case of the Brothers, the Cuban government showed patience, giving repeated warnings to the State Department through 1995 and into 1996. Cuba took this tolerant approach despite the October 1976 terrorist air tragedy that anti-Castro exiles had previously inflicted. At that time, two terrorists with strong links to covert US agencies blew up a Cubana Airlines passenger jet carrying 73 people.

Orlando Bosch, a fanatic anti-Castroite who co-authored that mission, now lives comfortably in Miami. In 1991, George Bush (41) gave him special dispensation to live there despite his long history of violent acts. Overruling objections from the FBI, Bush bowed to influential Cuban-American Republicans who had pleaded Bosch's case, calling a 'patriot'[72] this man who had fired bazookas at commercial targets in the United States and blown up an airplane.

Luis Posada Carriles, Bosch's co-author on the airline caper, worked for the CIA in the 1960s and early 1970s. The US government rehired him in the 1980s despite his terrorist past. His south Florida Cuban-American patrons bribed Venezuelan authorities to allow him to break out of prison. According to Lieutenant Colonel Oliver North's notebook, the late chairman and guiding force of the Florida-headquartered Cuban American National Foundation, Jorge Mas Canosa, allegedly paid $50,000 to the Venezuelan prison boss to spring Posada. He immediately went to work for North, Mas' buddy, to help supply the Nicaraguan Contras.

Posada today sits in a Panamanian jail cell with three other violent Castro-phobes on charges of conspiring to assassinate the Cuban leader when he visited Panama for a head of states meeting in 2000.

The fact that President George W. Bush has declared his intention to rid the world of terrorists has apparently not had an impact on the US government's view of Bosch and Posada, who enjoy world-class terrorist ratings. 'He who harbors a terrorist is as guilty as the terrorists,'[73] Bush said on several occasions. The double standard rhetoric does not appear to bother him when he warns other nations about the dire consequences of harboring terrorists. Indeed, Bush the President and Jeb Bush the Florida governor have apparently exempted anti-Castro terrorists from the general rules regarding terrorism.

Some anti-Castro Cubans who have spoken openly and proudly of their violent strategies still use Florida as both a residence and plotting headquarters. In case anyone doubts Orlando Bosch's ongoing intentions, listen to his own words in a different era. In 1979 he proudly proclaimed, referring to his fight to liberate Cuba, that: 'You have to fight violence with violence. At times you cannot avoid hurting innocent people.' He has never renounced that tactic. In a December 12, 2001 *Miami New Times* article (three months after 9/11) Bosch told reporter Kirk Nielsen, 'When they attack this guy, some innocents will be killed,' referring to the military assaults the United States would launch two days later in the hunt for bin Laden. 'It's like Churchill said: "War is a competition of cruelty."' According to Nielsen, Bosch admitted in early December to shipping explosives to Cuba.

Castro, in an October 6, 2001 speech in Havana's Revolution Square, raised the apparent contradiction in US anti-terrorist policy. 'We have the right to ask,' Castro declared, 'what will be done about Posada Carriles and Orlando Bosch, the perpetrators of that monstrous terrorist act [the 1976 airliner sabotage] … and about those who planned and financed the bombs that were placed in the hotels in [Havana], and the assassination attempts against Cuban leaders, which haven't stopped for a minute in more than 40 years.'

The anti-Castro terrorists have not limited their damage to Cuban targets. They have struck repeatedly in the United States, sometimes killing US citizens and others in what has become a love of violence.

In 1970, according to the FBI, members of the Cuban Nationalist Movement (CNM) bombed the Fifth Avenue Cinema in New York where my documentary film *Fidel* was being screened. Several weeks later, the same group burned down a theater in Los Angeles where the film was to have shown. In 1974, CNM activists bombed the Center for Cuban Studies in New York. Sandra Levinson, its director, narrowly escaped death.

In the mid and late 1970s, Cuban Americans who promoted dialogue instead of war against revolutionary Cuba also suffered from terrorism. Eulalio Negrin, a reconciliation advocate, was assassinated in New Jersey. Carlos Muñiz, a travel agent who arranged charter flights to Cuba, was gunned down in Puerto Rico. In Miami, Emilio Milian, a popular radio commentator had his legs blown off in an assassination attempt. Milian had opposed violence as a response to Castro.

So, as President Bush warns other nations of the consequences of harboring terrorists, he and his Florida governor brother harbor a list of men who have done and swear they will continue to do terrorism against Cuba. By contrast, the convicted Cuban 'spies' did no terrorist acts. Rather, as the trial evidence shows, they thwarted terrorism.

After September 11, Americans should understand what Cubans felt when unauthorized planes entered their air space. But the government prosecutor or judge in the case of the five spies ignored such feelings. Cuba sent those men to Florida to defend itself against US-based terrorists because US authorities had not fulfilled their police function. Does a terrorist need to have a first name of Ahmad or Muammar or a bin before his last name before US authorities rate him as a serious threat?

US officials have refused to include logic in their terrorism context. Fresh from victory over the Taliban, the Bush administration basks in a kind of asymmetrical imperial triumphalism. What a strange group of conservatives in the White House, who stray far from the path of Edmund Burke, the grandfather of modern conservatism. 'You are terrifying yourself with ghosts and apparitions,' warned Burke, 'whilst your house is the haunt of robbers.'[74]

'THE COUP LACKED PROFESSIONALISM!' THE EXPERT SAID*

Because the Senate refused to confirm him as Assistant Secretary of State for Western Hemisphere Affairs, Bush named Otto Reich to that post as a recess appointment. In January 2003, he demoted Reich to a minor position in the National Security Office. When the April 2002 coup in Venezuela occurred, however, Reich presided over US policy for the region.

SUNG TO THE MARINE CORPS ANTHEM

From the unpaved streets of Teheran
To the Guatemalan hills
We have punished those who disobey
We invade and then we kill

We will fight the corporate battles well
We will hold the poor at bay
We will proudly bear our imperial tag
We're the US CIA
(Lyrics by G. Bush, written for *Skull and Bones*, just for fun)

On Monday, April 15, 2002, a CNN Spanish anchor asked a Venezuelan 'expert' why the coup had failed.

'Lack of professionalism,' the professor pompously replied. I thought he might have meant the US Assistant Secretary of State Otto Reich's lack of experience in organizing such affairs. Reich has had ample experience as a professional in lying and twisting information, but not much in the way of coup making. As shaper of public opinion in Reagan's Office of Public

---

* Originally appeared in *Progreso Weekly*, April 25, 2002 and later in *CounterPunch*. I watched the news of the Venezuelan coup unravel on *CNN en Español* in Mexico City.

Diplomacy, Reich routinely lied about US involvement in writing assassination manuals, mining Nicaraguan harbors and ultimately about the facts of the Iran-Contra scandal.

Perhaps, I thought, the expert alluded to the CIA and Pentagon's employment of novices. But since CNN identified the man as a professor, I speculated that he thought the conspirators should have gotten PhDs in coup making at the Fort Benning School of the Americas (recently renamed the Defense Institute for Hemispheric Security Cooperation) before attempting their dirty deeds in Caracas. Latin American military officials, I presumed, could only qualify for such advanced graduate studies if they made a straight A average in their 'how to torture' courses.

Other CNN 'analysts' offered profound wisdom: 'this should teach Chavez that he can't exclude minorities,' or 'people's patience wore thin over his high-handed methods.'

A euphemism like 'minority' of course mean the ultra rich; people losing 'patience' signifies that the Venezuelan millionaires and the Washington national security gang had had enough of Chavez's heresy about helping the poor.

Not just CNN, but all mass media reached new depths in misreporting the class nature of the Caracas coup. Yet, during the few days before the 'prestige' press had to eat crow and admit that its reporting, comments and editorials did not coincide with the facts in Venezuela. I, like millions of others throughout the world, suffered feelings of desperation and anger.

Mexico's *La Jornada* called events correctly: a military *coup d'état*. Their reporters used on-the-scene sources. Most of the media accepted the undocumented line from the Caracas Chamber of Commerce and the State Department: the elected President Hugo Chavez had resigned after a powerful military–civilian alliance had exerted its rightful authority.

Sure, some cynics had predicted the coup on that 1998 day when Venezuelan voters overwhelmingly chose Hugo Chavez as their president. By invoking the term 'Bolivarian Revolution,' conjuring up the image of the Latin American liberator, Chavez signaled the onset of class war. He represented the 80 per cent poor people against the small gang that has claimed the lion's share of Venezuela's wealth and controlled its traditional political parties. This elite band has ruled (looted) the country for more than four decades.

Before Chavez pushed through a new constitution in 2000, he and his popular forces held and won a series of elections to change the rules. The wealthy and the corrupt, having lost at the ballot box, began to call Chavez 'anti-democratic' for practicing democracy. Among the wealthy and privileged minority who claimed the name 'civil society' (invoking the anti-communist dock workers' revolt in Poland) one found privileged union leaders, businessmen, church officials, and of course the owners of the mass media outlets who presented Chavez not as an elected president, but as a dictator, probably a communist, and certainly a friend of terrorists.

In two years, the President's popularity (according to the anti-Chavez pollsters) eroded from more than 75 per cent to less than 50 per cent. But analysts did not ascertain whether the drop in his popularity was due to his not delivering rapidly on some reform pledges related to the betterment of the poor, or to the media hype that painted him daily with deeply antipathetic colors.

'Realists' repeated the dogma that the United States would simply not permit the presence of another case of serious disobedience in the Western hemisphere. Cuba's Fidel Castro, in the *Guinness Book of Records* for his 43 plus years of naughtiness, had taught the national security gang in Washington its lesson: no more mischievous behavior in our sphere—from the right, left or center.

Recall that even arch reactionaries like the Dominican Republic's Leonidas Trujillo (1961), moderate reformers like Brazil's Joao Goulart (1964) and, of course, radicals ranging from Chile's Salvador Allende (1973) to the Nicaraguan Sandinistas (1990) fell victim to the CIA's punishing department. The covert tactics have included assassinations, coups, economic destabilization and psychological warfare; well, let's just call it state terrorism.

CHILE

Logically, CIA efforts to overthrow popular governments have always included attempts to influence the mass media. In 1970, while making a film in Chile, I witnessed parts of the 'destabilization' operation that began even before Dr. Salvador Allende won his plurality in September of that year. After the election, as the CIA hatched plots to prevent Allende's inauguration, I occasionally dropped into Santiago's Hotel Carrera bar. Invariably, well-dressed Chileans would whisper that Allende had advanced syphilis. Others would confide that he was a homosexual, a sex tool of Castro, a love slave of Brezhnev, intent on turning over control of Chile to Moscow.

I almost gagged at the grossness of the anti-Allende cartoons in the right-wing press (they controlled the majority of the Chilean media). I observed a campaign of planned violence, beginning with the October 1970 murder of the army chief General Rene Schneider, by Patria y Libertad, a gang of fascists hired by the CIA, as the Agency admitted to the Senate's Sub-Committee headed by Senator Frank Church in 1975.

The 'destabilization' continued through Allende's three years. By paying some labor leaders to call strikes in strategic sectors (like trucking and banking) and by imposing economic hardships on Chile, the CIA 'destabilized' Chile's economy. The CIA also provided a daily flood of lies and distortion about the nature of the Allende government and its agenda. Allende's goal was to better the lot of the poor working people, urban and rural, through legislation enacted under the existing Constitution. The CIA propaganda charged Allende with turning Chile into a Soviet satellite.

When the various and combined tactics failed, the Chilean military, aided by Washington, resorted to a bloody coup. The US navy played a crucial role, monitoring the traffic emanating from military bases so as to ensure that the coup makers could quickly dispatch any Allende loyalists.

September 11, 1973 stands for many Chileans as a day comparable to September 11, 2001 for Americans. Chilean air force jets fired rockets into the president's office building and tanks blasted away at the revered Moneda Palace as troops surrounded this symbol of democratic government. Then the military junta that grabbed control from the people began kidnapping, torturing and exiling political opponents—a campaign of terror backed by Washington.

After 17 years of Pinochet-led fascism, 3,190 Chileans had died at the hands of the terrorists whom Washington had helped into the seat of government. Tens of thousands had experienced the systematic and routine torture administered by Pinochet's repressive agencies.

JAMAICA

In 1976 and again in 1980, while making films in Jamaica, I had a déjà vu experience. In the bar of the Hotel Pegasus in Kingston, a Jamaican businessman told me that the Prime Minister, Michael Manley, was a homosexual. Another informed me that Michael was a Castro sex servant and dying of venereal disease.

Newspaper articles I had read a few years earlier in Spanish in Santiago's *El Mercurio* and other Chilean rags began to appear in English in Kingston's *Daily Gleaner*. They showed Manley as a Soviet and Cuban stooge. The violence and labor unrest, the rumors, the flight of capital—all the features of the Chilean operation, now appeared in Jamaica. In his first term, Manley had befriended the poor, struck up a friendship with Castro, his neighbor, endorsed Third World rights and rejected the conditions the multilateral lending agencies tried to impose on Jamaica. He also refused Secretary of State Henry Kissinger's request to condemn Cuba for sending troops to

Angola in 1975. Indeed, Manley supported the Cuban move. He paid for his independent behavior.

In July 1980, I sat next to Manley in his car when police agents told him that they had just thwarted an assassination attempt a mile up the road. Manley lost the 1980s election in an atmosphere of fear and violence—more than 1,000 people died in pre-election violence—generated by a CIA-backed campaign to 'destabilize' his government. He had tried to pursue an independent course, remove Jamaica from the dictates of the free market missionaries of the lending agencies and the US Treasury. He, like Allende, had designed legislation to aid the poor and promote healthy—not dependent—development. Some pro-Manley Jamaicans feared that, if he won, the violence and destabilization would increase. Some even confessed to me that they had voted against him because they feared that his victory would have meant more violence and some thought that the CIA would surely assassinate Joshua, as Manley's followers called him. (Like the biblical hero, Manley would blow his trumpet and the walls would crumble.)

In 1981, I visited a friend working in the US Embassy in Jamaica and she told me that on the night of the election after Manley had conceded to the CIA-favored candidate, Edward Seaga, the CIA station chief had invited the Embassy staff to a champagne party. He proudly opened his monster-sized safe on whose walls he had pasted the hundreds of articles, editorials and cartoons written or suggested by CIA personnel that had appeared in the Jamaican press.

So, when I read on April 12, 2002 that Venezuelan President Hugo Chavez had 'resigned,' I experienced the shock of understanding, not surprise. For two years, I had read about how organizations appeared mysteriously in the United States to protect or defend Venezuelan democracy. This alone would arouse suspicion. Such well-funded organizations never appear when right-wing dictators govern Latin American countries. When the US and its allied media ran consistently negative articles about Chavez, however, and ignored his accomplishments, my suspicions grew stronger.

From reading the *New York Times* or *Washington Post* how many Americans would know that Chavez had offered a democratic constitution, one he had designed in order to take institutional power from the traditional and corrupt political parties, which had shared power for decades? Did the reporters simply overlook this piece of Venezuelan history?

How many would have learned of Chavez's attempt to initiate land reforms that favored the small and landless peasants? Like the news blackouts on the above reforms, the newspapers also provided almost no coverage of his energetic environmental programs. Similarly, Chavez received scant press attention for his campaign against corruption, the hideous process by which Venezuela's political and business class had stolen the nation's patrimony.

Unlike his shady predecessors, Chavez invested in education for the poor and tried to increase their share of wealth. He also struggled to get more oil revenues for Venezuela and by taking a tough position inside OPEC (Organization of Petroleum Exporting Countries) he did succeed in raising revenues. In tandem, Chavez committed heresy by opposing the free market order. He used the government—a sin—to promote employment and offer credits to the poor and to women, and stepped on the toes of the rich when he insisted that they pay taxes.

The picture that the respected media painted of Chavez characterized him as something between a populist fascist and communist dictator who ruled because he adored power and practiced extreme media censorship. Not even feature stories appeared appealing to western feminists who would have applauded Chavez's appointment of women to high governmental posts. The sheepish US media repeated Otto Reich's briefing cliché, that Chavez represented yet another example of a power-hungry mad commy utopian bent on destroying his country's economy.

Then came the coup, portrayed in Washington and reported by the media as a democratic move to re-establish democracy and sanity and avoid inevitable and bloody class war. On April 11, the richest classes, backed by Washington, mobilized as many as 200,000 people who, in the name of democracy, defended the integrity of Venezuela's oil company, PDVSA, whose management Chavez had dismissed for failure to use its resource equitably for the poorest Venezuelans. Previously, the media had broadcast incessant advertisements for the impending march and the business groups had used their offices to set up telephone trees. They employed peer pressure to produce a massive outpouring: Chavez's enemies. And this minority, representing the old and corrupt order, marched for hours through busy streets in Caracas.

Then leaders of the march took a detour from their stated route in order to confront a few thousand rallying Chavez backers who had gathered in front of the President's office. Predictably, the clash became physical. Shots rang out from police, demonstrators and Chavez supporters. Snipers on buildings fired into the crowds. People died.

The plan, concocted between conspirators with the full knowledge—at the very least—of the highest authorities in Washington, went into effect. A few military officials seized Chavez. They apparently named—or else God did—Pedro Carmona, the Chamber of Commerce President, as provisional President and the media dutifully reported the events as if Carmona had magically appeared to restore democracy instead of destroying it.

As the *CNN en Español* anchor interviewed Carmona she somehow avoided asking him the obvious questions: 'The Venezuelan people elected Chavez. By what authority are you President?' Or, 'What happened to the Vice President, who the Venezuelan Constitution says should replace the President if he resigns?'

The next day, when Chavez supporters took to the streets in their hundreds of thousands and, unlike in Chile, key military units swore loyalty to the elected President, the coup fell apart. Lack of professionalism indeed! The people who voted for their President decided not to allow the filthy rich and the Washington interventionists to alter their destiny as they had done to so many Latin American peoples. And the majority in the military acted like professionals.

Once restored to the presidency, Chavez commented on the media and diplomatic subterfuge. He could have been referring to Reich. 'This is nothing new if you understand that they are imitating Goebbels, who in Adolf Hitler's time had the task of repeating a lie until it seemed true,' he said.[75]

I think it appropriate that hence forth when Reich or his ilk mention the word 'democracy' at a press conference reporters worth their salt should audibly pass gas—or at least emit a Bronx cheer.

We will spread our lies around the world
In the press and TV screens
So our president won't have to use
The United States Marines

(G. Bush in an attempt to win a contest for best official, but classified, lyrics for CIA rallying anthem)

Part V

Cuba—The Last Holdout

RELIGION, REVOLUTION,
MOBILIZATION AND ASSASSINATION:
43 Years After Echeverria*

In the museums hang portraits and photos of liberator José Marti and Fidel in the Sierra Maestra in 1957–58. Some of the actors who made the revolution write their memoirs and the government continues to celebrate the important battles and transforming laws—mostly 1957–75—that changed life on the island. A significant sector of the youth, however, seems both uninspired and deeply indifferent to this history. Like typical young Americans, they strive to consume.

On March 13, 1957, Jose Antonio Echeverria led a group of revolutionary students in an attempt to assassinate dictator Fulgencio Batista. They failed. Today, Cubans still commemorate the historic effort. Fidel Castro usually speaks on that occasion and refers to that noble but vain effort.

He has always implied that, unlike Echeverria's assassination model for political change, his guerrilla war strategy prevailed, because it was appropriate to the time and place. Underlying Fidel's guerrilla war model lies his idea of perpetual popular mobilization. As Julia Sweig insightfully analyzes in *Inside the Cuban Revolution*,[76] her 2002 book on the politics of the insurrection, by late 1958 Castro and the band of revolutionaries who had come together in a life–death commitment had already mobilized a substantial sector of urban Cubans against the Batista government—months before the guerrillas took over the reigns of power. And Castro has maintained mobilization as the core of his political process ever since.

Fidel has also criticized the anarchist assassination method as a flawed strategy because it targets one man, not a system. Ironically, the key counter-revolutionary organizations adopted the failed assassination strategy. Fidel used his enemies and the bully pulpit of state power to become both the political maestro and a religious figure.

In early January 1959, less than two years after Batista's police murdered Echeverria and some of his comrades, Havaneros filled the streets to greet the triumphant band of long-haired, guerrilla warriors that Castro had formed and led. The hated Batista with his entourage had fled to the welcoming arms of US officials in Florida, where some of them would plot against the new government.

Castro quickly answered the question on the minds of most Cubans: what would the new government do? He had already created a myth-sized

---

* Originally appeared in *Progreso Weekly*, March 21, 2002. Written on the 55th anniversary of Jose Antonio Echeverria's attempt to assassinate Cuban dictator Fulgencio Batista.

reputation by miraculously leading the vastly outnumbered and out-gunned *barbudos* (bearded ones) to victory. Indeed, how could a few hundred poorly armed and trained men defeat an army of 50,000 men, supplied by the United States? And, given the proximity of US power, how could Fidel continue to pursue revolutionary and anti-American policies and get away with them?

On January 9, 1959, Fidel Castro himself had entered the capital, after stopping in several cities on his trek westward from the Sierra Maestra. He had enthralled the applauding crowds in each stop with a heroic discourse of justice and independence. But now, in Havana's Camp Colombia, as Castro directed his words toward persuading rival revolutionary groups to disarm, an extraordinary phenomenon occurred. Several white doves fluttered around the orator and one, miraculously, landed on Fidel's shoulder.

For the *babalaos*, the high priests of Santeria, Cuba's popular religion, the landing of the dove signified that the gods had spoken. Fidel had gained the stature of a religious figure: Obatalah, symbolized by the white dove.

According to University of New Mexico sociologist Nelson Valdes, Obatalah dominates human minds; he stands for education. He can infect and cure people, possesses immense moral strength, hates money and uses the standard of justice to chart the course of his people.

In Santeria street speech Santeros use 'the horse' to refer to Obatalah. Within days of the dove incident, Fidel's name on the street had become *el caballo*. His charisma became popularly sanctified. Recall that charisma refers to having god-like attributes.

But this affirmation by the informal religious leaders of Cuba hardly diminished Fidel's practical political perspective; indeed, it strengthened his political prowess. In 1959, one didn't need Sherlock Holmes to deduce Washington's apprehension toward revolution—the most disobedient form of political behavior.

The clever Fidel delayed some of the impact of the inevitable counter-revolution force by providing respectable cover for his revolutionary agenda. He appointed to his cabinet politicians politically acceptable to Washington and refrained from direct confrontation with the United States in his early public speeches. Real power, as all serious analysts and members of the official cabinet observed, remained in the hands of the guerrilla leaders, like Fidel himself, his brother Raul, Camilo Cienfuegos and Che Guevara.

But revolutionary momentum quickly eroded the façade of respectability. Within weeks of the triumph, Fidel proclaimed an urban reform that reduced rents. In May 1959, he enacted an agrarian reform designed to limit the vast acreage held by sugar barons and cattle ranchers, including US owners like King Ranch of Texas and the American Sugar Company. As he began the reorganization of Cuba's productive agriculture, he also touched the sacred core of capitalism: private property.

The predictable scenario then unfolded. Much of the Cuban upper class and those associated with them had already fled, screaming 'the communists have come.' Those 'respectable' members of Castro's formal government resigned, most of them realizing by mid 1959 that they had no real power and were being manipulated by Fidel to cover his truly radical moves.

President Dwight Eisenhower, already grouchy from two major heart attacks, interrupted his golf game long enough to order the CIA to overthrow Cuba's revolutionary government, an order similar to ones he had given to knock off governments in Iran in 1953 and Guatemala in 1954. The CIA's Cuba formula meant recruiting an army of anti-Castro Cubans who had fled to the United States during the first year and a half after the revolution and then staging an invasion to overthrow and replace the Castro government with a US stooge.

In April 1961, when the proverbial egg broke at the Bay of Pigs, the yolk landed on President John F. Kennedy's face. Not since the Alamo had US-backed forces suffered a defeat from Latin Americans. Kennedy sought revenge. He and his brother, the Attorney General, Robert Kennedy, formulated plans to use exiled Cubans to assassinate Castro, and carry out a campaign of terrorism against Cuba's economy and society.

But assassins do not have an easy time with Obatalah. Fidel claimed in 2001 that the CIA, the Mafia and members of the violent Florida-based exile groups had made more than 600 attempts on his life. Recently declassified US documents reveal that the CIA had indeed backed thousands of terrorist missions against Cuba including assassination.

Over 43 years, ten US presidents have tried to isolate Fidel, waged psychological and, according to Cuban sources, even used chemical and biological war to damage his regime. For over four decades the United States has tried to strangle Cuba's economy with embargoes. The Soviet Union provided Cuba with generous aid and trade conditions.

In 1992, two years after the Soviet collapse, Pulitzer Prize winning *Miami Herald* columnist Andres Oppenheimer's book *Castro's Final Hour* gave new meaning to the words final and hour. Fidel, he had argued, faced a nascent opposition movement led by General Arnoldo Ochoa, whom Fidel had therefore executed for supposed narco-trafficking.

Oppenheimer's unfortunate title indicates that the American cognoscenti had expectations of Castro's rapid demise. Oppenheimer's argument, like those inside the US national security apparatus, failed to understand both

Fidel's deeply entrenched status in Santeria's cosmology and his incredible prestige in Cuba. In addition, Oppenheimer lacked any credible evidence to support his thesis.

In 2000, eight years after Oppenheimer's book was released, Castro showed how he could use political judo against his enemies. He turned the Elian Gonzalez struggle into an opportunity to re-mobilize an exhausted and demoralized nation and win a major political victory in the process.

In late November 1999, a US fisherman spotted six-year-old Elian floating in an inner tube in the ocean near the Florida coast. His Cuban mother and her boyfriend, who had taken the boy with them on an unseaworthy vessel, drowned on that Thanksgiving Day.

While Elian recovered from exposure in a Miami hospital, his Miami-based great uncle claimed legal custody of the boy, despite the fact that Elian's Cuban father demanded his return to Cuba. Despite the overwhelming legal and moral arguments for returning the boy to his father, the 'keep Elian here' movement managed to sustain the case for seven months. It became the cause célèbre for the anti-Castro hardliners in south Florida. Victory would demoralize Castro, they argued, deflate his power and lead to the fall of communism in Cuba. Revelations that Elian's great uncle had been arrested for DUI four times in Florida since 1990 and had child molesting charges against him in Cuba seemed to make no difference to the hardliners who insisted that returning the child to Cuba meant giving him to Fidel Castro.

Finally, in June 2000, after many court proceedings, the Attorney General, Janet Reno, ordered Justice Department officials to raid the guarded house of the great uncle, seize the boy and return him to Cuba. The decision caused great bitterness against both Reno and the Clinton administration, a bitterness that surfaced during the 2000 election when some of the fiercest of the 'keep Elian here' crowd reappeared to help intimidate the south Florida vote counters after the presidential recount was ordered.

Unlike the April 1961 Bay of Pigs, the fight over the little boy brought US majority opinion, which included Clinton and Reno, onto Fidel's side. Fidel won yet another battle and remains unchallenged at the helm.

The *babalaos* discuss the issue of which *orisha* will replace him. But, on the practical side, the island's economy has taken a hideous battering, from the slump in tourism following the 9/11 events, from a vicious hurricane and from the low market prices of sugar and nickel. The pervasive US embargo and travel ban persist, but nonetheless Cuba proudly points to its continued low infant mortality rate, about half of Washington DC's. The economists and political observers who once predicted certain collapse for Cuba's peculiar socialist experiment now talk of other things. But the 'utopia on earth' notion that Obatalah once offered to his people has also faded and some of the socialist values associated with the Cuba of the 1960s and 1970s have eroded with the everpresent force of the dollar and tourism.

As Cubans commemorate the anniversary of Echeverria's futile assault against Batista, a few of Castro's enemies still contemplate assassination as their only viable political tool. Their two-pronged strategy involves killing the leader and contributing money to the US political system to buy influence and ensure that no change occurs in US policy.

A plot hatched in Panama to whack Fidel by Luis Posada Carriles, Guillermo Novo, and other notorious terrorists in 2000 demonstrates the ongoing belief in the kind of violence that Echeverria had vainly attempted. The 'violent ones' in Miami still have powerful support from 'respectable' organizations like the Cuban American National Foundation, which retains easy access to the White House.

Indeed, thanks to right-wing Cuban-American influence, George W. Bush has become the tenth president to promise to bring Fidel down. This is an unbalanced contest. In a fair debate, Fidel would check his brains at the door so they could start even. Imagine, Obatalah doing battle with a moronic pretender to the American throne!

A CUBAN DIARY: PART I*

I arrive in Viñales, located in Pinar del Rio, Cuba's western province, after a two-hour drive from the noxious fumes of Havana, emitted by the oil refinery. Fidel Castro has just ordered all nooks and crannies to be zapped with some foul chemical so as to eliminate the dreaded Aedis Egipsis, the mosquito that haunts the Caribbean and whose bite causes dengue fever which, in its extreme form, causes serious illness and even death.

Nestled in a postcard setting, the tourist hotel overlooks a valley filled with manicured fields of tobacco leaves and palm trees, with farmers guiding yokes of oxen pulling ancient wooden plows. Seated at the next table, a middle-aged woman, dressed in an expensive but plain lace dress, with a high collar and long sleeves, pronounces, in a voice resembling Margaret Thatcher's:

'I find this place just like China. I hated it, you know, but it fascinated me.' I listen and watch in disbelief as the man seated across from her, presumably her husband, dressed perfectly for the tropical heat in a navy

---

* Originally appeared in *Progreso Weekly*, February 21, 2002. I traveled to Havana in early February for a brief visit.

blue blazer, starched shirt and public school tie, mumbles his assent. Perhaps all those layers shield him from mosquitoes?

I imagine people like these nouveau-upper-class English tourists in the 1920s visiting their colonies in Africa, sipping their *mojitos*, or whatever the native drink was, and smiling disdainfully at the dark-skinned waiter vainly intent on extracting a large tip from parsimonious vacationers.

This is one view of 'revolutionary' Cuba, 2002, a country that has come to rely on generally stingy and judgmental European and Canadian (less so) visitors, some of them unfortunately drawn to the island by the lure of gorgeous young women and men—or even girls and boys. But even more important than tourism for the Cuban economy are the million plus Cubans living in Florida and elsewhere. Indeed, remittances from Cubans living abroad to members of their families who live on the island total more than $1 billion dollars a year. These dollars end up in Cuba's central bank.

Ironic? Fidel's foremost political enemies have become the mainstays of the economy they swear to destroy. Not only did Fidel, from 1959 on, induce the United States to import his most ardent foes—people who now cause problems for the US instead of for him—but his eternally disobedient presence itself continues to provoke Washington. The irrationality of US–Cuba policy literally pokes citizens in the eye.

In a recent *60 Minutes* episode, Armando Perez Roura, one of Miami's leading Castro-hating radio talk show windbags, argued that the US trade embargo and travel ban had to remain intact as necessary measures so that the hated 'dictator' would not get one American cent. Yet this same Castro-phobe admitted that he, like many of the decent, family-loving, Castro-hating Cubans living abroad, regularly sends his brother on the island $300 remittances. Otherwise, he opined, 'my brother would starve to death.'

Most of the those who donate to Castro's treasury, via members of their family who spend the money at government-owned stores, refuse to acknowledge this obvious political incongruity. Together with tourism, remittances from Cubans living mostly in the United States make up Cuba's main sources of foreign income. Sugar has dropped to a distant place on the foreign income earning chart.

I remember a Cuba that from 1960 through the mid 1980s harvested sugar cane as its cash crop and had almost no tourists. Instead, the late Soviet Union provided the island's population with basic needs, neither luxuries nor the kind of subsidies that could even mildly suggest that consumption could offer a viable way of life for a sane Third World society.

Now, tourism, the necessary but very double-edged sword, has offered its devilish temptations to Cubans and the shiny glitter of individualism beckons a people whose heroic sacrifices helped change the destiny of several African nations and indeed altered the course of history in our own hemisphere.

I watch the English tourists stroll down the country road in Viñales and chat with the farmer whose tobacco plot adjoins the hotel land. He will, of course, try to sell them his own hand-rolled cigars for a much lower price than charged in the stores or by the street hustlers in Havana, who offer to the tourists either fakes or cigars stolen from the factories. They, like the farmer, need dollars to survive in the modern Cuban economy. Later, sitting on his back porch, I sip the sweetest grapefruit juice from his tree that I've ever tasted. I ask the farmer to assess the current situation.

The 65-year-old man wipes his very tanned and wrinkled brow and smiles at his wife who has served the fabulous libation. 'My six kids have all graduated from the university, my dozens of grandkids are all in school. But like her,' pointing to his wife, 'I was born here in Pinar del Rio [the province with choice tobacco soil] and got no education.' He lights one of his own 'tabacos' and continues: 'A few years ago, I was diagnosed as diabetic. Twice a day I have to inject myself. It costs nothing. Sure, there are shortages, especially in the cities and towns, but we small farmers understand that life means uncertainty and hard work. I have no complaints,' he smiles at his wife, whose face characterizes someone with gripes.

The stuffy, upper-class English tourists, for one thing, apparently drove a very hard bargain for the cigars and behaved as if the old couple were lesser people, 'as if they were superior to us,' the wife scowled. 'Who do these people think they are?' she asked rhetorically. 'You shouldn't have sold them anything,' she scolded her husband. He smiled at his wife's pride, her dignity. 'We don't need their $10,' she snorted, referring to the price they paid for 25 first-class cigars.

But in fact they did need the dollars to buy necessities for their grand-children—items the state used to provide before the Soviet Union, Cuba's sugar daddy for three decades, collapsed.

Today's Cuba represents the last semi-viable socialist country or island in a sea of turbulent capitalism. Fidel still preaches the old values in his speeches, which subsequently get reduced to billboard slogans and sermons on the daily television round table. Socialism, revolution, anti-imperialism— words that put a glaze over the eyes of many of Cuba's youth who think of the United States as paradise. These kids feel deprived because in their early childhoods they still received most of what they needed from the state. Now the state has had to reduce its subsidies and people complain. But most mature Cubans realize that their free healthcare and education, with all of their problems, mean more than a long shot at becoming a millionaire in the United States.

I think of Cuba's continued survival after the Soviet breakdown as a kind of miracle. Up until now, Cubans have not discovered great reserves of oil nor found strategic mineral deposits. Cuba's government has refused to make major concessions to the greedy multinational investors looking to exploit both workers and resources. It still provides people with a small part of their monthly needs—albeit less than a third of what they received when the Soviet Union provided Cuba with its beneficence. Cuba continues to offer scholarships to Third World youth who want to study medicine and Cuban doctors serve noble causes abroad and still treat the Ukrainian kids who suffered radiation poisoning from the April 26, 1986 Chernobyl disaster.

'This place is totally unrealistic,' a Cuban-American complained to me at the airport, referring to the difficulties Cuban government officials placed in the path of potential investors like himself. I agreed.

Cuba seems like an airplane in a decade-long holding pattern, with no clear plan of how or where to land yet determined to convert non-convertible material into fuel. It's far from perfect, but who in Washington would have bet ten years ago when the Cuban economy seemed headed for Hell that Cuban socialism under Castro would both survive and offer gradually improving material life to its citizens?

A CUBAN DIARY: PART II*

On my way to interview the Cuban Vice President, Ricardo Alarcon, I asked the cab driver to pick up a middle-aged woman waiting for a bus. The woman wore a facial expression of interminable suffering that reminded me of the model in Edward Munch's *Silent Scream*.

'I've been waiting almost an hour for the *guagua* [bus].' She reports that she does this twice a day. '*No es facil* [it's not easy],' the woman says about life in general, the cliché that Havaneros repeat almost as often as they do '*ay, que calor!* [gee, it's hot!]' in the predictably baking summer months.

The tortured look vanishes from her face as she thanks me for the ride and immediately informs me and the driver that she works in a hospital and earns 300 pesos a month (about $13 a month). She bakes and sells pies and cakes to supplement her income. She drops a suggestion that I could come and buy some right now and after I'd tasted them I'd never want a

---

* Written on January 29, 2003, after returning from a brief visit in early January to Cuba. Appeared in the July *LA Weekly*. Since 1978, the *LA Weekly* has run investigative and opinion pieces alongside showbiz news, what's happening in Tinseltown data and kinky personals.

Twinkie again. 'In my neighborhood, everyone says my cakes are the best. You could bring one home to Miami to your wife. You're married?'

I tell her where I live and that I'm married.

'Oh, California,' she says, disappointed.

She began her after-work job because her son in Miami stopped sending her money less than a year ago and this, she explains, has made her desperate.

'He says he has no money because he got laid off from his job, but I know him, that no-good ingrate. I'm certain he's spending money on whores.'

The cab driver enters the conversation.

'Lady, I don't know him or you, but why do you think that way? Look how you aggravate yourself. I used to worry myself because my brother stopped sending me money. Well, now I make enough. Think of the positive things in your life. That's what I do. I'm sure your son loves you and will send you remittances as soon as he gets his job back.'

She sighs and nods in agreement. 'Sure,' she says. 'You drive foreigners around in a taxi and make dollars. I help sick Cubans and get pesos.' The driver smiles. We arrive at her destination. She thanks me and offers me and the cab driver coffee if we want to come up to her apartment. We politely refuse.

'Come and visit any time,' she offers. 'Don't be strangers,' she says waving warmly with a smile on her face. The cab driver then gives her and me his address and makes a similar invitation to both of us.

I realize that I have engaged in a ten-minute conversation about intimate personal affairs with two strangers inside a taxi in a foreign country. The driver tells me he came to Havana seven years ago from Camaguey, a province in central Cuba, because 'I couldn't make a living there.'

He was a veterinarian and 'sometimes I miss practicing my vocation, but you can't live on 300 pesos a month.'

'Anyway,' he says, 'Havana is more interesting than the countryside.'

I told him that I had heard that farmers live well in Cuba.

'Some of the small farmers have made out well, but those on state farms and cooperatives don't do well.' And, he added, 'there's a lot of theft of animals and machinery. The police all went to the places where the tourists go to protect them, and get the drug dealers, so rural areas have practically no law enforcement.' He shrugged his shoulders. '*No es facil*,' he repeated. 'But not everyone wants to run away to Miami,' he sneered.

'So, what's your secret of survival,' I asked, 'aside from the dollars you earn driving?'

'*Hay que tener fe*,' he said. Literally this means 'you must have faith.'

Another cliché, I think to myself. He's turned to religion. I pay the driver. He looks at me as if I'm dense and without smiling clarifies: '*fe significa familia en el extranjero*.' Faith means having family abroad. He drives away. The joke remains.

Irony infuses conversation. Previously, I had dined with Javier, an electrician who lives in Santo Suarez, a working-class neighborhood. He described another common Cuban pun to illustrate how people cope with the vicissitudes of daily life in the post-Soviet period.

'Remember how many people left during the Mariel boatlift?' (In April 1980, some 120,000 Cubans left from the port of Mariel in boats and came to Florida.) 'At that time, as a member of the Young Communists, I participated in "*actos de repudio*" [acts of denunciation held outside the home of the person leaving] and screamed "*traidor*" [traitor] at those "scum" going north. Now, those same gentlemen and ladies return here as tourists, stay in fancy hotels that won't let us in and we shout at them when they come on the street with what sounds like the same slogan. But instead of *traidor*, we yell "*trae dolares*" [bring dollars].'

Laughter helps people through the day. Cubans have witnessed a dramatic deterioration of living standards since the 1980s. But most of those over 40 also realize that they still enjoy benefits that few other Third World people receive.

I saw some dirty clinics and schools in need of repair (a Fidel-sponsored 'fix the school' program began last year). But even in their deteriorated condition Cuban health and education services stand far above those in most Third World countries. Also, Cubans pay little or no rent, receive about one fourth of their minimum food needs from the government and get countless other services and benefits that other Third World peoples don't even dream about.

But because Cubans compare themselves to their relatives in Florida or New Jersey rather than to neighboring Haitians or Dominicans, they maintain a high level of irritation over the vicissitudes of their lives. Indeed, hundreds of Cubans risk their lives each month trying to cross the 90 miles of ocean water in smugglers' boats or makeshift rafts. Many of these are young people who fantasize about an Edenic life in Miami—if the US coastguard doesn't intercept them before they put a toe down on US soil.

Once having touched US territory, a Cuban walks a straight and rapid line to a green card, unlike any other immigrant. Thanks to this Cuban Adjustment Act of 1966, which gives special privilege to Cubans, almost a million have migrated to the United States. Hiding under the camouflage of 'political refugees,' most of these migrants seek better economic opportunities. And, unlike Haitians who also flee in boats through dangerous waters and Mexicans who risk death in the desert to cross into US territory, the Cubans arrive—those that don't drown or become shark food—in good health, have good teeth and high levels of education and skill.

The anti-Castro Cuban lobby has perpetrated the myth that all Cubans—except for Fidel and his cronies—want to come to the United States. Well, give or take 10 million, I conclude on my 100th trip to Cuba since the onset of the revolution.

Like Alarcon, into whose office I step inside to wait, some of my old friends belong to the same informal fraternity that formed in the early 1950s to overthrow the Batista dictatorship and build an independent Cuba. Most American journalists don't understand that hundreds of thousands of Cubans pledged their lives for this task that began in 1868 in the first war to liberate the island from Spain. Indeed, these nationalists still feel the painful frustration of loss in the 1898 (Spanish-American) independence war—when Cuba exchanged dependence on Spain for dependence on the United States. They also relate to the failed uprisings throughout the first half of the twentieth Century—each one suppressed by US force or threat of force. In 1953, for instance, the 26th of July Movement arose, named after the day in 1953 that Fidel chose to attack Cuba's second largest army base in Santiago, Cuba. In Fidel, Celia Sanchez, his long-time political companion wrote to her father in 1957, 'we have at last found our *caudillo* [strong leader].'

Most of the old frat members have died or retired; some continue to serve as government leaders, like Fidel himself (aged 76 at the time of writing) and his slightly younger brother, Raul (73); others write their memoirs or serve as advisers to government departments. The fraternity also recruited heavily in the 1960s and 1970s. Millions of teenagers came to understand their life's mission when they joined the literacy brigades to teach peasants how to read or studied and served abroad. When Cubans say, 'I served in Angola' (between 1975 and 1988), they do so with pride, unlike the mixed emotions carried by the statement in America, 'I served in Nam.'

Most Americans don't grasp the fundamental fact of Cuban politics: that perhaps a million or more Cubans have made a life-long commitment to the shared ideals of independence, sovereignty and social justice. However imperfect life became at certain points, especially during the 1980s when the flaws in the Soviet model made themselves dramatically clear, and whatever the difficulties with government policies in the post-Soviet period, these committed Cubans know they have participated in the transformation of their island.

A few of the fraternity members that I've known from the early 1960s felt 'betrayed' and defected. Some even took up violence as their means of opposition to the process after Cuba took on its communist coloration in

1960–61. Some just got tired and dropped out, living their lives without political involvement. But many of the adherents suffered the trials and tribulations of the decades of socialist experimentation and nevertheless remain attached to the ever evolving ethics of equality, social justice and internationalism. All Cubans have criticisms, but the faithful continue to insist that pragmatism and opportunistic solutions to immediate problems of the economy and social structure would ruin their ideal.

As a retired military officer assured me, Che Guevara remains the icon because, 'socialism has to mean the making of a better human being. My children and grandchildren will have ingested values they learned in school, at home and everywhere in Cuba and that will make them noble people. Well, at least that's what my life has been about. We'll know for sure after I'm dead,' he smiled.

Ricardo Alarcon Quesada has been a leader of the revolutionary fraternity for 40 plus years. While he wrote his PhD thesis on Rousseau at the University of Havana, he also joined the underground movement that fought parallel to and in coordination with Fidel's mountain-based guerrillas. He sits back in his less than comfortable chair in the reception room at the National Assembly Office. We sip watermelon juice as we talk on my January 25 visit. In addition to his vice presidential role, he also serves as National Assembly Speaker. He doesn't take off his cheap blue windbreaker. Like all Cubans he feels vulnerable to the temperature now that a rare cold snap that has hit the island.

'In Miami, I understand it went below freezing. Is Miami part of the United States?' he asks rhetorically. 'Events in Miami would astonish Americans living in other parts of your country. It's the only place where you can plot terrorism, against Cuba of course, and get US government support. These days the leaders of your government have made security so important an issue that they use it to scare people every day. At the same time, they permit lawlessness and create an absence of security in the segregated republic of Dade County in Miami, where you can do anything to try to destroy Cuba—apparently, with help from the US government. It's a payback to that Cuban exile mafia living in Miami' (referring to their 'help' in the Bush brothers' campaigns and vote counting in 2000).

According to Alarcon, Cuba had sent infiltrators to Florida to penetrate organizations that were plotting terrorism against Cuba because the FBI refused to stop them. In 1999 five were convicted of espionage and sentenced harshly.

'The US has not fulfilled its obligations to fight terrorism,' he says bitterly. 'Instead, it is protecting terrorists. The most quoted phrase by President Bush refers to this idea. "Those who harbor terrorists are as guilty as the terrorists themselves." Agreed. Is the US government innocent of protecting terrorists? It's simply shocking that your country right now in the midst of its big war against terrorism has convicted terrorists who have killed Americans in downtown Washington DC, New York City or Miami walking around as free men. Those people were freed by Attorney General Ashcroft in July and August 2001. They watched TV on 9/11 as free men and didn't have any concern that they could be taken into custody for questioning, because they know that they engage in terrorist activities that will continue to have support from the same government.' He also emphasizes that the terrorists protected by the US government have drug connections, an issue that has become pressing in Cuba.

'Look,' says a 55-year-old teacher, whose husband works as an auditor. 'We have serious problems here, especially drugs right now. But most of us don't think that just because daily life stinks we can jump on some smuggler's boat for a few thousand dollars and escape to the paradise of the United States. We have an obligation.'

She serves black syrup in a small cup. 'You like the coffee?' she asks. I nod my assent as the caffeine and sugar combine in my stomach to send a nervous tic to my cheek, while my knees start shaking.

She tells about four killings in her Havana neighborhood. 'Debts,' she explains. 'With this crazy drug nonsense young people become addicted quickly and run up debts and then get killed just like in the American movies. We have to stop this quickly.' Her opinion coincides with the official line on drugs.

Her daughter, a 30-year-old architect, chimes in. 'It's not that simple, Mommy. Things have changed. The adolescents are bored and anxious. Foreigners bring drugs, Cubans distribute them and poof, you have a criminal drug problem like in the United States.'

Her mother insists on quick and severe justice, prison terms for users and long prison terms for dealers and death for the kingpins.

Another friend had visited someone in prison and told me: 'Coño, there are thousands of teenagers locked up. All for drugs. I didn't realize it was this bad.'

The government has urged farmers to report on people growing, selling or using drugs in the countryside. On January 10, 2003, *Granma*, Cuba's official newspaper, ran a letter from a farmers' association pledging rural Cubans to 'make this fight permanent, keeping ourselves alert, denouncing and condemning any case detected or known, whether it be growing drugs, possession, trafficking or consumption in our countryside.' The farmers also promised to look at the coastal areas for drug deliveries. Any farmer caught dealing or growing would lose his land and serve a long sentence to boot.

'Recently,' the editorial reported, 'the illicit use of drugs has grown, although at a much lower rate than it has in other countries.' The government line has been to blame tourists for bringing the nasty goods. Indeed, as I came into the airport a cute spaniel sniffed me and my bags and then went on to the other arriving passengers.

Since 1995, the government reported in *Granma*, Cuban police had arrested more than 250 foreigners, including more than 50 Americans, for importing illegal drugs. To underline the seriousness of the problem, *Granma* on its front page defined drugs as a threat to 'the health, ethics, dignity, and values that we have created in the face of danger.'

Drugs, like large-scale prostitution, came in inevitably with tourism and Cubans understand that they will not easily return to their pre-tourist, drug-free ambience. Tourism provides the Cuban economy with vital cash flow.

So, what keeps Cuba afloat? One can wander the streets of Havana and, except for those in a few industrial areas, it's difficult to find people engaged in productive work. Lots of them ride on the infrequent camels (hump-shaped trailers attached to semis) and lots of people hang out and provide services and work for the government.

Yet, in 2002, Cuba reported a 1.1 per cent increase in its gross domestic product, while the rest of Latin America fell by 0.5 per cent. Cuba accomplished this modest growth despite a drop in tourism of more than 5 per cent and a fall in the prices of her major exports. In addition, Cuba lost out when, after the April 2002 coup, Venezuelan President Hugo Chavez could no longer guarantee Cuba cheap or free oil. On top of that Cuba suffered the affects of violent hurricanes that hurt its tobacco and other crops. And the US embargo still raises the costs of her imports.

From 1994 to 2001, Cuba grew 4.1 per cent; the rest of Latin America about 3 per cent. Writing in the January 3, 2003 *La Jornada*, the Cuban journalist Angel Guerra contrasts Cuba with Peru, which in 2002 grew by 4.5 per cent, the most in Latin America. Yet half of Peruvians live in dire poverty and more than one quarter are unemployed. Peru has an 11 per cent illiteracy rate, while in Cuba literacy increased to over 97 per cent. Cuban infant mortality continues to be lower than in the United States. A Cuban leader claimed that in 2002 the government placed 50,000 computers in Cuban classrooms and reduced class sizes to a maximum of 20 pupils per classroom.

For these material reasons and for ideological and patriotic ones as well, the vast majority of Cubans don't think about migrating to the United States. Also, one shouldn't discount inertia. The difference between Cubans and other Latin Americans, however, is that Cubans have high expectations and, ironically, a greater understanding of their rights than most Latin

Americans—the rights to food, shelter and clothing, free education and medical care, and the right to retire with a decent pension. Note, I don't mention free press, speech or politics.

Cuban leaders face the problem of how to keep socialism alive on one island in a sea of capitalism. Indeed, capitalism itself has fared poorly in Latin America. Argentinians, once the richest in the lower hemisphere, now have among the highest poverty levels.

As I leave on the 40-minute flight to Miami on the Continental Airlines charter, I see the rich land below, the smoke from the fires where the weeds are being burned. I see Havana's skyline and the immense stretch of the city. For 43 years I have observed Havana grow in population, from about 1 million to over 2 million today. Yet, people in Havana produce little and consume—albeit not as much as they would like.

My old friends and associates, some of the relationships dating back to the 1960s, don't want to move to the United States. They do want to travel and earn some dollars so they can live more comfortably. But they prefer their Havana routines, part of which means figuring out how to get specific kinds of food or replacement parts for household machines and cars.

Previously, I used the metaphor of Cuba as a country in a holding pattern. But so are most Third World economies. Aside from Cubans' superior access to good healthcare and education, they also enjoy greater safety and security than their Caribbean island neighbors. Their leaders have inspired several generations throughout the world by achieving redistribution of wealth in the face of US attempts to destroy them. This aging fraternity brought revolution and independence to the island. But many of their own youth are dramatically unimpressed with these past performances.

For three decades Cubans danced on the world stage as no other Third World people have, making history in southern Africa and Latin America, producing artists, scientists and athletes and sending doctors all over the world. Now independence means loneliness and Cubans, I think, are frightened of being alone. Their days of history-making are over, at least temporarily (Cuba may assume leadership of the Non-Aligned nations' movement in 2006), and they have joined the rest of the Third World people who bear the enormous brunt of centuries of colonial rule.

This year or next, or the one after, the US government will inevitably submit to the pressure of large multinational corporations, who will spend more than the powerful mafia in south Florida, and the embargo will disappear along with the travel ban. Cuba will then have to defend itself against the rapacious capitalists and vulgar tourists who will want to Americanize a country that has escaped McDonald's—and McDonald Douglas—for 44 plus years.

Part VI

The Move to War

After the 1979 Iranian Revolution and the rise of fundamentalist Islam to state power, the US Persian Gulf–Middle East policy dance became more complicated. The United States felt obligated to aid Iraq, a genuine enemy of Israel, in its 1980–88 war with Iran, lest the Ayatollah Khomeini's regime should dominate the region. Helping Iraq develop and then deploy chemical weapons in the war, however, did not mean that US policymakers had etched a temporary Washington–Baghdad entente into anything permanent.

When Iraqi President Saddam Hussein ordered his army to annex Kuwait in 1990, President George Bush saw his chance to launch the US into unquestioned predominance in 'the new world order.' He dropped all pretenses of warmth toward Iraq and created a convenient demon to take the brunt of what has become the violent ritual of policy change.

But Bush (41) did not want to take the risks required to dispatch Saddam. It might look less than politically perfect to have US troops occupying a distant country while campaigning for re-election in 1992. So, the United States withdrew and left Iraq under sanctions so that the UN would 'punish Saddam.' The Iraqi President didn't miss a meal but the Iraqi people have suffered horribly. In addition to causing hundreds of thousands of deaths through deprivation, throughout the decade President Clinton regularly and routinely bombed 'targets' in Iraq's 'no-fly zone,' created by Washington and London as western territory protected by the Allies.

In July 2002, ten months after 9/11, George W. Bush declared that Iraq once again stood as the pre-eminent and immediate threat to the region, the United States and the world.

I traveled to Iraq after Bush had made it clear that he intended to go to war to remove Hussein from power.

FIVE DAYS IN IRAQ—BEFORE THE WAR*

We share the one-hour Gulf Falcon Air 747 flight from Damascus to Baghdad with dozens of Iranian women pilgrims on their way to the holy city of Kerbala. They used knife sharpened elbows to get first in line through Syrian immigration and then onto the plane. 'Saddam Hussein would be better off using them than weapons of mass destruction,' quipped *New Yorker* writer Milton Viorst, a member of our delegation.

The Mission to Baghdad is led by Congressman Nick Rahall, Democrat from West Virginia, and former senator James Abourezk from South Dakota, both of Lebanese descent. They intend to try to convince Iraqi leaders to readmit UN weapons inspectors and thus expose President Bush's flimsy pretext to make war. This is a reasonable and logical political step, albeit it may prove unrealistic given President W's Groucho Marx-like (see *Duck Soup*) but very unfunny intention to make war.

Part of me wants to see Saddam pay for killing Iraqi friends I made in college. Part of me wants him to pay for his cruelty to all his opponents, especially to the Kurds, a people he has relentlessly persecuted. But I hate the idea of US planes firing missiles at urban targets. I also feel a little frightened.

As we arrive at the Baghdad airport and get ushered to the VIP lounge past the scowling Iranian pilgrims, I don't see a single armed cop in the airport. The Iraqi officials eagerly inform us that they have arranged for us to inspect supposed sites of weapons of mass destruction. Abourezk tactfully assures our handlers that we wouldn't know a soap-making factory from an anthrax production plant. So we avoided that pitfall. The Iraqi handlers look pained. I feel little sympathy for them.

I rely on Scott Ritter, a former Marine Corps officer and also a Republican. He belonged to UNSCOM, the United Nations Special Commission, created in 1991 to inspect Iraq for weapons of mass destruction. Ritter, who looked all over Iraq, claims that Iraq had no significant weapons of mass destruction and was 'qualitatively disarmed' when the team left in 1998 under UN orders, just days before Monica's then boyfriend renewed bombing raids during Operation Desert Fox. Saddam did not kick them out.

On the late night ride into Baghdad from the airport, temperature around 95 degrees, but pleasant enough in the air-conditioned Mercedes-Benz, I see no indication of war preparations. Our handlers, Wadah, a 40-year-old Foreign

---

* Originally appeared in *Progreso Weekly*, October 2, 2002, and later in *Anderson Valley Advertiser* and *Canadian Dimension*. Written after returning from filming a congressional delegation visit to Iraq during September 15–20. The film is called *Iraq: Voices from the Streets*.

Ministry official and his younger and beefier assistant Mustafah, behave politely. The chauffeurs all look like bodyguards, squat, tough-looking men in their early forties who have the hard-calloused hands of karate fighters.

As we see in the street and in the *souk* (market), Iraq is a Third World country, hardly a clear and present danger to the United States. Its military prowess, greatly exaggerated by Bush the First, has fallen to less than a fifth of what it was during the Gulf War. Iraq has virtually no navy and a very small air force with antiquated planes. Bush has yet to explain how Iraq could pose a threat to US national security. Well, we all know Saddam is evil and therefore, I suppose, capable of anything—like putting chemical weapons in the stomach of a flying camel and programming the humped animal to land in Washington.

At 2 a.m., I involuntarily step on George Bush's face as I enter the Al Rasheed Hotel. Some mosaic tile designer has inlaid 41's portrait on the floor of the hotel entrance. 'George Bush War Criminal,' it says underneath.

'Welcome,' the smiling doorman says. The bellhops who have carried my bag a few feet from the elevator to the room demand tips. I offer a dollar for the guy. One of them snarls nastily. I give him five more. I go downstairs to the cafeteria. 'Welcome,' says the manager, 'welcome,' says the waiter. At this rate tipping will bankrupt me. We finish snacking at 4 a.m. I'm too excited to sleep. I look out the window at the lights of Baghdad. Could this have been the same room from which Peter Arnett's crew shot the light show put on by American bombs and missiles and Iraqi anti-aircraft fire at the onset of the 1991 Gulf War? Only street lights twinkle; no flashes against the black sky. I now understand that those flashing lights, bombs and missiles hitting targets that CNN transmitted to the world were equivalents of jumbo jets hitting buildings, some of which had people inside. I try to put myself into the position of a Baghdad resident who had to withstand the explosive and incendiary power of thousands of tons of bombs over a prolonged period of time. My admiration for them rises. I wonder if I could take it—a pounding worse than the V2 rockets gave to London.

At 9 a.m., the Minister of Health, Dr. Omid Medhat Mubarak, a former cardiologist, clad in his spinach-green government uniform, tells us how the twelve-year-old UN sanctions interfere with the integrity of the Iraqi health system. 'It's not the UN,' he says, 'it's the American and British delegates overseeing the oil for food program who veto our medical purchases.' He explains with a grim, mildly depressed look on his middle-aged face how by refusing one part of the cocktail of chemotherapy drugs you nullify the whole treatment and by omitting one part of a surgical hookup you invalidate the whole procedure. 'It destroys the integrity of our healthcare system,' he concludes.

As if to prove his point, we're whisked to a nearby pediatric hospital where we see children in beds suffering from leukemia and other cancers. I see Abourezk trying to cover a tear as he observes blood oozing from the mouth of a frightened and whimpering five-year-old Kurdish girl from the north. She clings to her mother. According to the doctor, they live too close to fragments of a bomb made of depleted uranium dropped by the US Air Force during the Gulf War. Because of the UN sanctions, Iraq cannot buy medication to treat her. At least that's what the pediatrician told us.

'My daughter's about that age,' Abourezk says. I recall that the former secretary of state Madeleine Albright, when asked whether the price of over 500,000 Iraqi children killed by the sanctions was worth it, replied, 'this is a very hard choice, but the price—we think the price is worth it' (see note 16). I never understood exactly what price Ms. Albright had to pay.

The children's mothers, however, have paid dearly. They sit on the sides of the beds, fanning and comforting their cancer-ridden offspring. They implore us to help them get medicine. We stare. With IVs stuck in their toothpick-like arms, the emaciated kids cry or whine softly. After seeing six of them, the nausea hits me—and I worked for years in a hospital.

What blame do Saddam and company carry for the plight of these kids? He invaded Kuwait and they pay the price exacted by US power. I bet Saddam and the Iraqi leaders don't go without medicine or surgical procedures if they need them. The victims in the pediatric hospital are poor. So what's new?

The doctors drone on as did the Health Minister about the thousands of bombs the American planes dropped during the war and afterwards in populated areas, but mostly in the no-fly zones, areas arbitrarily created by the US and UK. The Pentagon claims that Iraq fires anti-aircraft missiles at the US bombers flying over Iraqi territory. Therefore, the US must retaliate with missiles or bombs. Later, kids play near those 'targeted' areas. Needless to say, the Defense Department assures us that depleted uranium is perfectly safe.

The worried mothers dressed in black, except for a Kurdish woman in a long grey dress, plead with us for help. Congressman Rahall, like Abourezk, shows emotion on his face. According to Tun Myat, UN Humanitarian Coordinator in Iraq, and Sanjiv Kumar, UNICEF Project Officer for Health and Nutrition, the under age 5 mortality rate in Iraq has increased from 56 per 1,000 in 1985–89 to 131 per 1,000 during 1995–99. The two UN officials also report that one in every eight Iraqi children dies before his or her first birthday, 60 per cent of mothers are anemic and one child in three suffers from chronic malnutrition. The sanctions have worked—but for what end?

It's over 100 degrees outside as our Mercedes limousines push their way through chaotic Baghdad auto and bus traffic. Exhaust fumes pour out and mix into the dusty heat. We visit a turbulent *souk*, in which peddlers and hawkers offer inexpensive local crafts, canned and fresh—well, sort of—food, plastic toys, electronic gadgets, CDs, video cassettes of X-rated movies and regular Hollywood fare.

The Iraqi middle class resorted to selling their personal and household belongings in order to buy food in the years following the Gulf War. I notice women wearing the traditional long black dresses, with the black shawls covering their heads, not their faces. A few wear only the *hijab* and occasionally I spy a woman donning western garb. About half the men sport the *dishdashas*, the long robe, with or without the *kefiya* on their heads.

Harold, a member of the group, stops at a rug merchant and begins the bargaining process in English. I interrupt to ask the merchant how he feels about the war. The rug peddler smiles. 'Why you want war? What good is from war? We have plenty of war. We know bombs. We know destruction. What we do to you?' Harold nods approval and the rug merchant immediately resumes his sales pitch. He makes a sale. As other people in the area grow curious and crowd around our group, our nervous handlers herd us back into the Mercedes.

We're set to see Tariq Aziz, the English-speaking Deputy Prime Minister and former foreign minister. Slightly built, with neatly combed gray hair and a trimmed mustache, this veteran Ba'ath Party man looks out at us through thick eyeglasses.

Rahall and Abourezk hold a private meeting with him while the rest of the delegation stare at Saddam Hussein portraits in the waiting area. In three hours, I've already counted eight different Saddam poses. I ask our foreign ministry guide how many there are. He glares at me scornfully. I say I liked the one of Saddam in the black derby holding a rifle in the air. He snorts. By the end of the trip I have stopped counting.

It becomes clear very quickly that this secular dictatorship has nothing to do with Islamic fundamentalism. You don't need Vincent Cannistraro, who headed the CIA's counter-terrorism office, to assure you that Iraq's links to Al-Qaeda are dubious. To rev up the war engines, the White House has been desperately pushing a bogus Prague meeting between September 11 villain Mohamed Atta and an Iraqi intelligence officer. Indeed, Czech President Vaclav Havel himself has denied that such a meeting occurred in his country.

One of our Foreign Ministry guides assures me with murderous intensity that an Al-Qaeda operative in Baghdad wouldn't last five minutes. Bin Laden, I'm reminded by our guide, offered to mobilize 100,000 fundamentalists to resist the Iraqi invasion of Kuwait so the Americans wouldn't have to come in. Unlike Saudi Arabia, Iraq has no religious police. The more myths dispelled about Iraq, the better, I think. I've seen women with ponytails in tight slacks walking next to those in long black robes.

The Deputy Prime Minister, Aziz, emerges from his office with Rahall and Abourezk, and then holds forth at length in a large conference room as Rahall presses the case for readmitting the inspectors. Aziz describes them as spies, a conclusion backed by Scott Ritter. 'And we didn't kick them out,' he reminded us. They left 'voluntarily under Clinton's orders two days before Clinton bombed us in 1998.'

Aziz, a man who appears to be in his early seventies, clad in his olive green uniform, sighs. Bush's UN speech threatened war even if the inspectors are admitted, he says, locking his fingers over his tiny paunch. 'America,' he says softly, 'is a threat to world peace. If Bush wants to change the regime in Iraq he must come into Iraq city by city and occupy each one. Everyone endangered by the invasion will fight.'

Abourezk interrupts to try to clarify Iraq's position on accepting the inspectors.

'We're doomed if we do [let the inspectors in],' Aziz said, wringing his hands, 'and doomed if we don't.' He shakes his head. We shake our heads. 'So you better don't,' he concludes. This avuncular looking Christian intellectual, in a predominately Muslim country, exudes a kind of frustrated fatalism. 'If you don't have guarantees that Bush won't invade why expose ourselves to foreign inspectors? They'll inspect military barracks, tanks, aircraft, and artillery. Why let them in if we're going to be attacked anyway?'

Aziz belongs to the fraternity of Ba'ath Party members who created the nationalist regime that overthrew the Revolutionary Command Council led by President Ahmad Hasan al-Bakr on July 16, 1979. Saddam, with his Ba'athist Muslim and Christian comrades, has ruled since then as the President and chief ideologue of Ba'athism, a kind of mélange of Pan-Arabist, anti-imperialist and anti-Zionist doctrine. Similar to nationalist movements throughout the Third World, the Ba'athists stressed true Arab independence from all forms of colonialism. But most of the nationalism of the 1950s, 1960s and 1970s, epitomized by Egypt's Gamel Abdul Nasser and Tanzania's Julius Nyerere, has disappeared. Indeed, Saddam's Iraq represents the strongest of the disobedient obstacles to US domination of the Middle East. I wonder if that's how the Iraqi people perceive Saddam? He may be a tough, cruel bully, but do Iraqis see him as a protector from the American bully? Or do many see him as the mother of all bullies?

In addition to his own palaces, he led his people to build a modern country, with a solid infrastructure—until the United States et al. bombed much of it into stone and sand during the Gulf War. In the years following the Gulf War the regime almost totally rebuilt the highways and hospitals, the water and sewage treatment plants, and pushed the economy into forward motion. And now, says Aziz, 'we who have done nothing to provoke or threaten the United States are about to be attacked again.'

'Why?' The question echoes from the lips of every street person we ask. 'Why you want war?' asks a rug merchant. 'Peace,' he screams into our camera.

As soon as people discern that we're Americans, they use their poor English to plead, beg, demand, exhort us to not bomb them again—as if a small US delegation had any more control over our government than they have over theirs.

That night we meet 'intellectuals,' a group of English-speaking men and women who discuss with us 'the situation.' Rahall and Abourezk stoically endure an anti-Zionist rant from a former Iraqi diplomat, a retired general, an English literature teacher and several other party-liners. The Zionist lobby runs America and the entire anti-Iraq scheme was cooked up in Israel. I wonder if the 'blame Zionism for everything' explanation comes from decades of propaganda or is it just that Iraqi intellectuals cannot conceive that the United States truly intends to enjoy 'full spectral dominance,' the words from the White House's new National Security Plan.

On Monday, September 16, we wander into the Sixth Iraq Solidarity Conference. Vladimir Zhirinovsky, the neo-fascist and anti-Semitic Russian presidential candidate, reiterates the Zionist-plot charge. 'Oil, oil and control by Israel lobby,' he shouts at me.

Later, our delegation visits a bomb shelter that took two smart bomb hits in the 1991 Gulf War. The government has converted the former shelter into a museum. During the war, our intelligent weapons transformed 408 women and children from flesh into ashes. The guide, Intesar, a beautiful and bitter neighborhood woman in her mid thirties, who covers her head with a *hijab*, states that 'the Pentagon discovered its mistake and four days after killing the people huddled in the shelter it said sorry. Too late.'

Inside, the photos of many of the deceased line the walls. Wires and bent iron rods that once reinforced the concrete dangle from the ceiling. 'This,' Intesar says, 'is what war does.' She points to what looks like the outline of a woman etched into the wall. The bomb literally burned her into the side of the shelter so that her image, with her clothes, remains embedded there.

The next day, as I still shake from both a nightmare that had me agreeing to help kill my daughter and the appalling scene of the bomb shelter that I feel produced it, we begin our feast of mosques. Our delegation has already seen Al Kadhimain, an enormous gold-painted structure in south Baghdad. Men and women enter this mosque like they do a subway station, only they kiss the door before entering or utter a brief prayer. Inside, whole families eat lunch or take naps, 'feeling their spiritual roots,' the Imam tells us. Outside the mosque on the busy street I see fast food places but no McDonald's or KFC as they apparently have built in the Holy City of Mecca in Saudi Arabia.

As we stare at the acres of King Nebuchadnezzar II's reconstructed palace, built in circa 600 BC, I begin to understand tradition. In the United States a 50-year-old house gets landmarked. Professor of Anthropology James Jennings, another member of the delegation, accompanies us and explains where the hanging gardens once hung, the spectacle that amazed all visitors. Jennings talks about how the kings designed their complex palaces and how they also made war and, like Hammarabi, issued law codes. He reads inscriptions still visible on the original bricks in ancient languages that predated Hebrew and Arabic.

Was Saddam much different from King N or from Hammarabi, who also eliminated opponents whom they deemed unreasonable? Hey, if they didn't, the opponents would kill them. That's been a political axiom in the region for a few thousand years.

Back in Baghdad, we rent a boat for a ride down the Tigris, one of the waterways along with the Euphrates that produced the Fertile Crescent, the source of agricultural wealth for Mesopotamia (land between two rivers). Kids dive into the river for a swim in the 105 degree heat. During and right after the Gulf War, raw sewage poured into the Tigris, polluting it. A man in a long white robe casts his net. A pesky jet skier revs his engine alongside the boat. Later, at dinner, on the banks of this biblical river we watch a boatload of teenagers rocking to hot rhythms, Algerian 'Rai' music, I'm told. Other boats pull alongside and people jump on board to join the party. The restaurant goers smile their approval. Hardly the kind of atmosphere that the Taliban would welcome, I think.

I had remarked earlier to Warren Strobel, the *Knight Ridder* reporter, that I had seen no preparations for war on the streets, no mass mobilizations, no parades of military vehicles; not even a demonstration. 'Yes,' he agreed, 'but how do you prepare for the leviathan?'

Finally, we see our first indication that Iraqi leaders are doing something to get ready for the imminent war. Wadah leads us to the National Museum and has angry words with people who appear to be its directors as we wait in the lobby with a crowd of unshaven men in *dishdashas* and *kefiyas*. They look surly and unfriendly, some of them casting downright suspicious stares at the US delegation. 'They are preparing for a civil defense exercise,' Wadah announces. 'So the museum is closed.'

'I assume that the guys who work there will defend the museum?' I ask.

Wadah shrugs. As I change clothes I see the TV in my room showing pictures of Iraqis preparing for civil defense drills. But, on the street, I've seen nothing but casual civilian life.

We have a session with Sa'doun Hammadi, the Speaker of the Parliament, in his well-furnished and spacious office. A University of Wisconsin PhD in economics in the late 1950s, the now frail scholarly-looking man, in a neatly tailored gray suit, repeats Aziz's arguments and offers numbers and facts on the perfidy of the weapons inspectors.

'UNSCOM,' he says, 'has sent 476 inspection teams to Iraq, with 3,485 experts, who inspected 3,392 sites and set up an ongoing monitoring system in over 365 sites, with 10,256 visits to those sites. They installed 130 sophisticated cameras plus 30 advanced inspection units. Iraq has no weapons of mass destruction. The allegation that we're building a nuclear bomb is a pretext for beating the war drums. The UN inspector who resigned in 1997 said Iraq was basically disarmed. Instead of lifting the sanctions we got missiles and bombs against our infrastructure.'

'We have no relation to Al-Qaeda, bin Laden or the Taliban, no link to 9/11. We're anti-terrorist. If war is made,' he says his voice in full throttle barely rising above a whisper, 'our people will fight. I personally will fight, but at the end of the road this adventure will fail and you can estimate what damage will be done to the United States.'

Hardly more of a threat to the Pentagon than the sharp-elbowed Pilgrims, Hammadi nevertheless reflects the anger of even the most reflective of officials. As he rises and walks slowly to the door, I notice the worry lines etched in his face.

In five days I have seen ancient palaces and mosques and the fascist-like modern government buildings in Baghdad. George W. Bush, who probably can't count the number of days since he last visited a library, prepares to authorize bombing of a place where libraries existed while Western Europeans were throwing rocks at each other. Does our geography-challenged President realize that another war here could destroy the cradle of civilization? Doesn't Armageddon refer to such an event?

On my last day in Baghdad, I chat with a woman with dyed blonde hair and tight pants. She runs a souvenir shop. She tells me she has just returned from a vacation with her Algerian live-in boyfriend to Barbados and Martinique and 'I could hardly wait to return home. I love it here.'

I ask her how she will respond if war comes. She shrugs. 'I am Christian,' she declares, 'and I love my President because he is strong and protects us. Without a strong president like him, we would be persecuted. All of Iraq would be chaos, disorder. I stand with him against Al-Qaeda, the Taliban, bin Laden and George Bush.' Her Algerian boyfriend grins in agreement.

The despotic Saddam, like the late Tito in Yugoslavia, simply does not permit ethnic or religious friction in public. What I have seen of Iraq confirms that the people are deeply religious, predominantly Muslim—both Shia (more than 50 per cent) and Sunni (less than 20 per cent)—but nevertheless have a secular society and government. Saddam's ongoing war against the Kurds in the north aims to crush their desire for autonomy. According to the government spokesman, he has no trouble admitting them as Iraqis. 'See the woman in the hospital,' he lectures. 'As a Kurd, she has the same right as all Iraqis to medical treatment.' The Kurds have taken a licking for wanting nationhood, from Iraq, Turkey and Syria. The United States has offered them support on several occasions, but always withdrawn it in the interests of regional stability or for some more banal reason.

The dozens of people with whom I speak refer to what they see as Bush's intention of killing innocent Iraqis and reducing their developed infrastructure to rubble as his father did almost twelve years before. To a person, they cannot see how Iraq threatens the United States. Indeed, they point out that none of their neighbors—even the recently invaded Kuwait—complains about them as a threat. So, for lack of another explanation, they fall back on the Zionist conspiracy. They don't get the nuance of US politics. Above and beyond achieving imperial dominance, the neo-cons' strategic goal, starting a war against Iraq will artificially pump up Bush's poll ratings—along with oil prices—and keep corporate scandals, economic problems and healthcare crises, for which he and his party are blamed, off the front pages.

The day before we leave Iraq announces it will readmit the UN inspectors without conditions. The Iraqi foreign ministry official tells us that our trip has been successful. Abourezk smiles and says, 'Yes, with a little help from Nelson Mandela, the Arab League and UN Secretary-General Kofi Annan, all of whom strongly urged Saddam Hussein to accept the inspectors.'

British MP George Galloway, also attending the Iraq Conference, rejoices over the news. 'The fox is shot as we say in Britain,' he declares. 'It means you must stop the hunt if the fox is dead.' Then he says that the United States presents a frightening posture to the world. 'Naked imperialism,' he calls Bush's behavior.

Abourezk, also delighted with the news that the Iraqis have taken his and Rahall's advice on the inspectors, hopes that Congress will now show some backbone. Within two days he finds out that the Senate Majority leader, Tom Daschle, who once worked for him as a Senate legislative aide, has all but rubber stamped Bush's demand for sweeping military powers. Abourezk agrees with Galloway. 'It's naked power,' he says and 'George Bush refuses to take yes for an answer.' Galloway, a left Laborite, says we should refer to Shakespeare for clues as to why George Bush (43) blindly pursues Saddam Hussein.

Our delegation says goodbye to the friendly and tip-crazy hotel staff and to our guides and chauffeurs and gives sighs of relief that the sharp-elbowed Iranians are nowhere to be seen. As we watch from the plane to Damascus and see the lights of Baghdad, I think about Abourezk's words. 'If we can remember the absolute horror we all felt on September 11, we can imagine such destruction being wreaked on the Iraqi civilians every day that American bombers drop their deadly loads.'

THE CHICKEN HAWKS' WAR*

A journalist asked President Bush what had priority, the war against terrorism or the war against Iraq? Bush, with that revealing look of bewilderment on his face, answered, 'Well, uh, hm, er, gosh, I'm trying to think of something funny to say.'77

If you have a very droll sense of humor, you'll chuckle over the fact that Bush's advisers have convinced the Prez that war against Iraq is not only divinely ordained, but politically opportune as well. These particular advisers share with the President a common life experience—or lack thereof: they have not seen military combat. Thus, some veterans describe them as Chicken Hawks.

The New Hampshire Gazette *defines chicken hawk as 'a term often applied to public persons—generally male—who (1) tend to advocate ... military solutions to political problems, and who have personally (2) declined to take advantage of a significant opportunity to serve in uniform during wartime.'*

Two years ago, Bush would have had trouble locating Iraq on a map; even today he cannot articulate a fact to support his bellicose crusade. One reporter asked him if this fixation on regime change in Iraq had become a personal crusade against Saddam. W did reportedly say that Saddam 'tried to kill my dad.' The charge has persisted for almost a decade. It stems from an alleged plot to kill Bush 41 on a 1993 visit to Kuwait, although US intelligence agencies have not revealed clear evidence to support the allegation. Nevertheless, those who draw the context around the box of debate have triumphed. People who have been rightly labeled as chicken hawks have successfully manipulated the very question at issue from: 'Is Saddam Hussein

---

* Originally appeared in *Progreso Weekly*, October 9, 2002. By September 2002, several reporters had observed that the leading advocates of war had not served in the military.

a viable threat to US security' into 'How best to deal with this urgent threat to US security?'

They have done this by repeating accusations that contain no facts, much less evidence that Saddam in Iraq has accumulated weapons of mass destruction that constitute a direct threat to US security and that Hussein's regime enjoys close links to the terrorist network, Al-Qaeda, thus linking the Iraqi dictator to the fiendish acts of 9/11.

In the course of this transition, officials of the Bush administration and their reliable lap dog, the British Prime Minister, Tony Blair, have repeated the claims but have yet to present the public with a fact. Bush, in his September 12, 2002 UN address, and Blair, in his 'Dossier' (later discovered to be plagiarized, written by a graduate student) of evidence presented to Parliament during the same month, used lots of 'probablys' and 'likelys.' When I asked a national security official to show me evidence of Al-Qaeda–Iraq links, he declared, predictably, 'that's classified.' Does that mean that only the national security elite and Saddam Hussein can share the secret? That the US public can't know what its supposed mortal enemy knows?

Listening to the administration warriors and AM radio talk show hosts, all of whom assume Bush's word is sacred, one could conclude that any hesitation about sending bombs and troops to Iraq constitutes liberal cowardice—if not downright treason. Yet if one looks at the war records of the leading hawks one sees nothing but poultry feathers. I can well imagine that talk show charlatans and senior officials in the Bush administration fall asleep every night dreaming about combat and carry memories of these glorious fantasies into work the next day. That's as close as most of these neo-cons pushing 60 on one side or another have gotten to real battle. Like the President himself, who managed to enlist in the safe Texas National Guard—and went AWOL for his last 15 months of service—the sons of the rich, famous and powerful avoided any dangerous postings.

In the 1960s, as Jim Lobe dramatizes in his September 6, 2002 'Chicken Hawks as Cheer Leaders' published by the Project Against the Present Danger, Dick Cheney ducked military service as he told one reporter because he 'had other priorities.' Donald Rumsfeld did his navy years between wars—no combat. Only Colin Powell, thought of as the dove of the Cabinet, knows war first-hand. Cheney's chief assistant, the feisty 'Scooter' Libby, took student deferments during the Vietnam War. The Deputy Defense Secretary, Paul Wolfowitz, and Peter Rodman, a defense intellectual and Rumsfeld cheerleader, have likewise never seen combat.

National Security staffer Elliott Abrams, the pugnacious prevaricator, assiduously avoided danger while advocating that others fight and die. The Under Secretary of State for Arms Control and International Strategy, John

Bolton, Lobe discovers, had 'medical problems' to keep him out of the Vietnam War. Bolton fights fiercely with his fowl mouth. Most of those who have taken the strident pro-war positions have never even had a fist fight. These cowards want the US military to knock over Iraq, Iran, Syria and Lebanon.

The baby-faced Richard Perle, who chairs the Defense Policy Board, waited out the Vietnam War at the University of Chicago. He then joined pro-Vietnam War Senator Henry Scoop Jackson's staff and made his reputation as one of the youngest of the defense intellectuals. Like Jackson, Perle made pro-Israeli policy an axiom of his discourse. Perle has become well-known for his aggressive mouth on TV talk shows, contradicting the flaccidity of his physical demeanor.

Republican Senator Chuck Hagel of Nebraska singled Perle out sarcastically as one of those whom he 'would like to be in the first wave of those who go into Baghdad.' Hagel described the chicken hawks as having 'an intellectual perspective versus having sat in jungles or foxholes and watched their friends get their heads blown off.'[78]

Ironically, we have watched three former chairs of the joint chiefs of staff state their dire misgivings at congressional hearings. Gulf War commander General 'Stormin' Norman Schwarzkopf and former Central Command head General Anthony Zinni, have expressed their serious doubts about Bush's war plans. The right-wing intellectuals who occupy high posts and have both ears of the President have drawn a scenario whereby US forces quickly and easily 'liberate' Iraq, get rid of Saddam and return control of the country to its happy people who adopt a US-style democracy and live happily ever after as part of the globalized world of production and shopping. They imprudently view the way in which Afghanistan was 'liberated' as the surefire method for solving the Iraqi problem.

They scoff at notions that US troops might have to occupy Iraq for 25 years or more, and they belittle notions that ethnic and religious groups in Iraq, some of whom have centuries-old traditions of hating and killing each other, would resume their old patterns as they did in the former Yugoslavia.

The chicken hawks mock the generals as knowing nothing about war, as compared with themselves who have not only read about war in serious books but have watched it on TV. Moreover, they have cast the 'chilling effect' net over opponents of making instant war. As members of Congress who had recently returned from Iraq sought to widen the debate, Republican Senator Don Nickles of Oklahoma, another non-combatant, picked up the chicken hawk line and accused his colleagues of sounding 'like spokesmen for the Iraqi government.'[79]

Such statements indeed help to keep the real issues, corporate scandals, the weaknesses of the economy, which include growing poverty and unemployment, the healthcare crisis and the very real issue of terrorism, from taking the front seat. The war against Iraq now requires nothing more than a Tonkin Gulf resolution or an incident like the explosion of the Maine—or maybe no provocateur at all—to set the world on yet another deadly course.

The US public needs to parse carefully the phrases of these chicken hawks and see if they can find a fact that could conceivably present itself as a cause for war.

COUNTERING AMNESIA: The Iraq Ploy and Resemblances to the Start of the Cold War[*]

Déjà vu! An Iraq scenario emerges similar to the script that led to the onset of the cold war. In 1946–47, British and American leaders invented an imminent Soviet threat to invade Western Europe. The British Prime Minister, Winston Churchill, coined the 'Iron Curtain' notion—referring to what the Soviet premier, Stalin, had symbolically draped over his 'empire' to seal it off—to begin the psychological war campaign. Stalin, known as 'Uncle Joe' during World War II became by 1947 'Stalin the Butcher,' a dangerous and nefarious foe. President Harry Truman and his coterie transformed the allegiances I had formed through World War II propaganda. *My Weekly Reader,* required for all grade school kids during that war, showed Stalin, Churchill and Roosevelt together in photos. The trio stood as the epitome of kindness and virtue—in contrast to Hitler, Tojo and Mussolini, the old axis of evil.

So too, in the 1980s, the US government had offered a helping hand to Iraqi President Saddam Hussein, who would act as their surrogate against Iranian fanaticism. In 2002, Bush charged Saddam with backing the fanatic terrorists, whom he had previously fought. In a literal pique of moral indignation, Bush also charged Saddam with violating the sacred resolutions of the worthless—well, at least irrelevant—United Nations!

However zany such speculations may have seemed to the factually enlightened, Bush's 2002 'axis of evil'[80] speech nevertheless set the tone and

---

[*] Originally appeared in *Progreso Weekly*, October 16, 2002, and later *CounterPunch*. When Bush repeated for the umpteenth time in October that Saddam had links to terrorists and possessed weapons of mass destruction, I began to recall events from my childhood, when the cold war myths were created.

context for future political discussion. Within months, the prestige media and political elite had substituted Baptist sermon language for political analysis. A White House speechwriter's imagination that attributed God's blessings to us and his curse on Saddam had become converted into axioms of policy. The issue became not whether Iraq might conceivably threaten US interests in the distant future, but whether to take unilateral or multilateral action to quickly combat the immediate threat.

Think back to the post-World War II years when US leaders repeated implausible charges that the Soviet Union constituted a 'clear and present danger.' Poised to attack Western Europe, alleged US and British leaders, the Soviets also aimed to subvert democracy everywhere—referring to communist parties in European and Third World countries. These dubious statements became the 'factual' basis for the cold war. The incessant propaganda campaign that followed the allegations contained no references to the real facts: the USSR had just lost more than 20 million dead and had 20 million more wounded; 200 cities had been demolished; and the country was suffering acute food shortages.

Yet within months the publicity machinery, with the unquestioning and obedient media playing its designated role, transmuted the false claims into truisms that in turn became the foundations of military alliances like NATO (North Atlantic Treaty Organization), SEATO (South East Asia Treaty Organization) and CENTO (Central Treaty Organization). SAC (Strategic Air Command) bombers flew round the clock missions with nuclear payloads and, from this demonstrably false premise, hundreds of domestic institutions developed to fight Soviet communism and eventually win the cold war.

This dubious legacy lives on. The national security agencies created to contain the Red Menace continue to thrive long after communism has collapsed. Ironically, Russia now plays an important role in the joint NATO–Russia Council, the very organ created to combat the Russian menace.

The cold war origins should serve as a warning for the present state of affairs with Iraq. But instead temporal atrophy seems to have gripped the US public. The media helps memory erasure by making no references to how the national security elites generated the cold war.

Similarly, the Bushies and Blairites have repeated *ad hominem* arguments against Iraqi leader Saddam Hussein who, because he committed horrendous crimes in the recent past like 'gassing his own people' in Halabja (he might not have done this particular crime, according to a January 31, 2003 *New York Times* op-ed written by Stephen C. Pelletiere, a former CIA senior political analyst on Iraq in the 1980s, who cited a US Defense Intelligence Agency study that asserted that it was Iranian gas that killed the Kurds at Halabja, not Iraqi gas), must by now have accumulated weapons of mass destruction and forged links with terrorists. Like Stalin, Saddam is a genuine black hat. That does not, however, mean that the United States must go to war against Iraq just as it did not need a half-century of cold war to deal with the USSR.

The missing links in the administration's argument are facts. Instead of supporting their claims with evidence, they rely on amnesia and hyperbole to bamboozle the public. They also count on obedience to authority to reign in the press corps. Questioning a basic policy, even one so bereft of fact and logic as the 'Iraq threat,' could mean negative career possibilities for a journalist.

We do not hear the press, for example, asking the President and his advisers about why US policy changed from being pro-Saddam in the 1980s to anti-Saddam in the 1990s. Declassified State Department cables and court records indicate that President Ronald Reagan and George Bush the elder as Vice President actually endorsed Iraq's use of chemical weapons against Iranian troops in the 1980s, which is today considered an unspeakable crime.

In 1983 Reagan selected Donald Rumsfeld, the perfect right-wing Republican, as his emissary to Iraq to explain to Saddam that, while the United States could not openly condone Iraq's use of poison gas, it would look the other way because Washington wanted to prevent an Iranian victory.

According to MSNBC on November 17, 2002, evidence of this agreement emerged from depositions taken in a January 1995 court case in which Howard Teicher, a National Security Counsel official who traveled with Rumsfeld to Iraq, states that both Reagan and Vice President Bush personally delivered military advice to Saddam Hussein, both directly and through intermediaries. In his affidavit, Teicher writes that the Director of the CIA, Casey, 'Personally spearheaded the effort to ensure that Iraq had sufficient military weapons, ammunition and vehicles to avoid losing the Iran–Iraq war. The United States supplied the Iraqis with billions of dollars of credits,' claims Teicher, 'and offered military intelligence and advice to the Iraqis, and ... closely monitor[ed] third country arms sales to Iraq to make sure that Iraq had the military weaponry required.'

In 1986, according to Teicher, President Reagan sent a secret message to Saddam Hussein telling him that Iraq should step up its air war and bombing of Iran. Vice President Bush delivered this message. At this time, both Reagan and Bush knew that Saddam had used chemical weapons and cluster bombs but nevertheless wanted to help him stave off the Iranian attacks. The US also assisted in facilitating sales of such weapons to Iraq, says Teicher.

On December 30, 2002 the *Washington Post* finally printed a front-page story by reporter Michael Dobbs that acknowledged that US companies with administration approval supplied Saddam with elements necessary for making his weapons of mass destruction.

Today, Rumsfeld's apparent memory loss about his 1980s mission as Reagan's conciliator allows him to convert into appalling crimes the very acts that he encouraged Saddam to commit—like using poison gas against his enemies. Rather, he testified to the Senate Armed Services Committee on September 19, 2002 that Iraq threatens 'its neighbors, the United States, Middle East and international peace and stability. It is a danger we do not have the option to ignore. The world has acquiesced in Saddam Hussein's aggression, abuses and defiance for more than a decade.'

What a change! In 1984, Rumsfeld, dealing with the same man and the same regime, delivered an encouraging message to Saddam: 'The [United States government] recognizes Iraq's current disadvantage in a war of attrition since Iran has access to the Gulf while Iraq does not [and] would regard any major reversal of Iraq's fortunes as strategic defeat for the west.'[81] In other words, the United States would support Iraq. Rumsfeld also discussed lifting sanctions to allow Iraq to buy military equipment.

In the August 18, 2002 New York Times, Patrick Tyler reported that in the 1980s a US official had stated explicitly after touring the battlefield area in 1988 that the Reagan administration did not consider the use of gas on the battlefield by the Iraqis a matter of deep strategic concern. But the press corps ignored Tyler's story and the Times did not follow up.

Likewise, the media did little with Rumsfeld's letter to the Secretary of State, George Shultz. Yet Rumsfeld's words contradict his current and downright dogmatic position. 'I said I thought we had areas of common interest, particularly the security and stability in the Gulf, which had been jeopardized as a result of the Iranian revolution,' wrote Rummy in the 1980s. 'I added that the US had no interest in an Iranian victory; to the contrary. We would not want Iran's influence expanded at the expense of Iraq.'[82]

In his 1993 memoirs, Shultz affirmed that reports of Iraq using chemical weapons began drifting in by December 1983. In March 1984, the State Department confirmed that Iraq had used lethal chemical weapons against Iranian combatants. United Press International cited a team of United Nations experts saying that mustard gas laced with a nerve agent had been used on Iranian soldiers in the 43-month Persian Gulf War between Iran and Iraq.

Amnesia when used in diplomacy can get tricky—if the press refers to it. For example, in 1990, after meeting with the US Ambassador, April Glaspie, Saddam assumed he had a US green light to invade Kuwait. Perhaps Ms. Glaspie believed that Saddam intended to recapture only the north-eastern tip of Kuwait, which Iraq had historically claimed and with good precedent. She told him that Washington would not see its interests threatened by his move into Kuwait, noting, 'We have no opinion on the Arab–Arab conflicts, like your border disagreement with Kuwait.'[83] But Saddam, not adroit in discerning nuance, took the whole enchilada. With his annexation of Kuwait, the modern demonization campaign began. Saddam gained himself the ultra-disobedient label.

When the US government decides to punish a disobedient former friend or client, stories, rumors and reports mysteriously appear that suggest that the ingrate has now become a black hat. And the public should rally around this 'hate whomever' campaign.

To convince the public of Saddam's malevolence in 1990, God provided the elder Bush with the Hill and Knowlton public relations firm. The PR spinners discovered a Kuwaiti princess who agreed to testify before Congress that Iraqis tossed Kuwaiti babies out of incubators. The media dutifully reported these horrors without checking. Weeks after the story had become major headline news, a reporter discovered that the princess never saw the events she swore that she had witnessed. Indeed, she had never left Washington and the events she described did not occur.

In order to deliver punishment, the US government also must show that the current incarnation of the Devil threatens us and his immediate neighbors. So, amnesia resurfaces. The administration orchestrated the media to change key facts about the past to make Saddam look more evil.

In 2002, for example, the prestige media said that Saddam had kicked out the UNSCOM inspectors in 1998. The very same media in 1998 reported that the UN ordered them to leave, because the US government had warned them that they intended to bomb and did not want to kill UN inspectors. According to Swedish diplomat Rolf Ekeus, an UNSCOM inspector, the Americans had used members of the inspection team as spies to track Saddam's movements in order, presumably, to assassinate him.[84]

The push to destroy Iraq marks the onset of America as the Rome of the twenty-first century, the sole and exclusive enforcer of its order. It's the chapter that will erase the last thin lines of the Republic.

This expansion that began in the eighteenth century with 13 colonies, and stretched across a continent, absorbing half of Mexico and hundreds of Indian nations, took on international proportions in the twentieth century. After World War II, the United States pursued the cold war for 45 years! In the course of that era, US troops fought dubious wars in Korea and Vietnam and scores of smaller skirmishes and covert actions.

In 1967, following the passing of the Tonkin Gulf Resolution by the Senate in 1964, Oregon's Wayne Morse remarked:

> We're going to become guilty, in my judgment, of being the greatest threat to the peace of the world. It's an ugly reality, and we Americans don't like

to face up to it. I hate to think of the chapter of American history that's going to be written in the future in connection with our outlawry in Southeast Asia.

That outlawry continues 40 years later in the Middle East.

BUSH TO LEAD COALITION OF THE WILLING— TO BE BRIBED AND INTIMIDATED— AND THE WARMONGERING*

'When the rich make war, it's the poor that die.'—Jean-Paul Sartre, a writer from the old Europe.[85]

'Turkey turns Chicken,' screamed a February 22, 2003 *NY Post* headline, referring to that country's reluctance to allow the United States to station troops there en route to attack Iraq. Turkey demanded more than $30 billion in bribes, er, aid, as a condition for US troop deployment at Turkish bases. It did not want credit, promises or IOUs. Cash, said the Turks. House Speaker, Republican Dennis Hastert, after months of slashing the domestic budget and raising money for the 2004 election campaign, swore that he'd personally vouch to the Turks for the dough. But the Turkish parliament remained unconvinced.

The Turks had learned from others to whom Bush had made promises. His erstwhile buddy President Vicente Fox of Mexico had given Bush two years of solid support, but when the time came for the US to make good on its side of the quid pro quo, legalization of some 3 million Mexicans living in the United States, Bush didn't understand the meaning of quo— or quid.

The guidelines for forcing administration policy on the public have become: 'You can bamboozle the jerks by scaring them half to death about imminent terrorist attacks or Saddam Hussein conquering the world. They'll back the Prez in war and keep the campaign contributions coming!'

The cowardly and obedient Colin Powell, his Secretary of State, provides Bush the veneer of decorum. The other heavies, Vice President Cheney, and the Defense chief, Rumsfeld, retreads from older administrations, pretend

---

* Originally appeared in *Progreso Weekly*, March 6, 2003. In answer to charges that the US was about to wage an aggressive war on Iraq all by itself, Bush announced that the US would lead a coalition of the willing. Of the nations who signed on, seven of them ended in 'IA,' as in Estonia, Romania, Lithuania, Bulgaria ... Bush pointed to his two willing European partners, England and Spain, to demonstrate that his aggressive war against Iraq was not imperialist.

to give him avuncular advice about policy, like how to gather a 'coalition of the willing' to fight the 'Hitlerian Saddam Hussein.' According to Christopher Dickey in the September 23, 2002 *Newsweek*, thanks to Rumsfeld, President Reagan's envoy to Iraq during the 1980s, 'America knowingly permitted the Iraq Atomic Energy Commission to import bacterial cultures that might be used to build biological weapons.'

West Virginia Democratic Senator Byrd read the Dickey article into the Congressional record and then addressed Rumsfeld.

'Mr. Secretary, to your knowledge, did the United States help Iraq to acquire the building blocks of biological weapons during the Iran–Iraq war? Are we in fact now facing the possibility of reaping what we have sewn?'

Rumsfeld quickly and flatly denied any such knowledge but promised to review Pentagon records. 'I suggest that the administration speed up that review,' said Byrd. 'My concerns and the concerns of others have grown.'

No wonder Bush and company don't want to talk about the past, whether it's drinking and drug-taking on Bush's part or Rumsfeld's role in helping the psychopathic Saddam Hussein acquire terrible weapons! Indeed, White House word spinners invented 'New Europe' and threw into it the ever-willing Australian government, a few easily intimidated and illegitimate Persian Gulf regimes, far-right-wing governments in Spain and Italy and the ever servile Tony Blair of England. At home, a percentage of the unthinking and frightened public accepted Bush's hyberbole for making war.

For more than six months, he has presented no facts that Saddam posed a threat to his neighbors, the region or the United States. Nor has he shown evidence of links to the terrorists who carried out the 9/11 deeds. According to the UN weapons inspectors, Bush presented false information about Saddam's supposed accumulations of weapons of mass destruction. Bush announced a pre-emptive war doctrine, including the possible use of nuclear weapons when and if he decided on its necessity. Those who listened to this new doctrine were shocked: it literally undoes all the law developed since the end of World War II. It posits that the United States could employ nuclear weapons if it simply suspected evil intent on the part of another state.

Bush's war plans have nothing to do with self-defense. He overstates or misleads because he seems convinced in his own mind that a fact (or a judgment, isn't that the same thing?) should produce absolute certainty. Iraq, he declared, represents a 'grave threat to the United States.' It's easier to act and sound dramatic than to study.

Think of the obvious implications of dispatching hundreds of thousands of troops and war material to the Persian Gulf! As preparations for war began, the CIA wrote to the Senate Intelligence Committee and advised it that Iraq would not likely launch an attack with weapons of mass destruction or share such weapons with terrorists unless Saddam believed that 'a US-led attack could no longer be deterred.'

Indeed, the CIA had concluded that Saddam would not attack the United States unless Saddam concluded that he had no other choice and he would 'exact vengeance by taking a large number of [American] victims with him.'[86]

On October 7, 2002, Bush justified his own bellicosity by explaining that 'the risk is simply too great that Saddam Hussein will use instruments of mass death and destruction, or provide them to a terror network.'[87]

Where, I asked myself, did he get these zany ideas? Look at the possible interests pushing for war: pecuniary and strategic oil, water, Israeli pressure to have Iraq as a place to 'transfer' Palestinians, the re-election campaign? Or just building a world empire without the money to pay for it?

Worse, why did the rest of the world accept them instead of laughing? The entire world is debating these loony notions in NATO, the media and the councils of state throughout the world. The UN Security Council and the world's mass media have all accepted a non-compelling issue—how to deal with Iraq—and elevated it into a primary place on the world agenda. What a triumph for an intellectually challenged president!

We have heard him say the silliest things and we now understand he does not allow his decisions to fall under the influence of facts and logic. Like the fabled Bourbon kings of France in the nineteenth century, he neither learns nor forgets anything. So, in his mind, the English are 'willing,' despite the fact that polls show some 80 per cent of the public opposed to war with Iraq without UN backing. Tough Tony Blair, the so-called Labour Prime Minister who has never labored, and the ultra-right-wing Spanish and Italian prime ministers, José Maria Aznar and Silvio Berlusconi, willing and eager to help Bush, might have to do so at their own peril if Georgie Poo doesn't hurry. Public opinion in Spain and Italy, like that in England and throughout Europe, manifested in the streets on February 15–16 when millions made it crystal clear: no war in Iraq.

Bush laughed the protests off, likening them to a focus group that looks at a Republican Party campaign ad. How do you reason with an alcoholic? No, you explain to him, millions in the street means a very strong expression of opinion, not a small group of selected critics looking at an ad to see if it can raise the 'negatives' of an opponent.

From the evidence, it appears that the impending war has a small minority of willing people and lots who will follow orders. Does Bush believe that thousands of Bulgarians, Poles and Lithuanians (those great new Europeans) will eagerly charge forth into battle alongside the US mercenary army—that's what a volunteer army means doesn't it?—in their quest to destroy the evil villain, Saddam Hussein? They may have to whack a few thousand or more Iraqi civilians to do it, suffer destabilization in the region, pay the ensuing high price for oil, and help Osama bin Laden—remember him?—recruit more terrorists, but that's the price of glorious war.

Those who think differently, like 'Old Europe,' meaning France and Germany, said Secretary Powell, 'are afraid of upholding their responsibility to impose the will of the international community.'[88]

Hey, Colin, I wanted to shout, the international community stated its opinion. The German and French leaders represent that will by leading the UN Security Council in a call for more and tougher inspections and exhausting non-military options. Indeed, it is the minority that has imposed its will on the international community! And they have done so in the face of expert opinion from their own military and intelligence officials. A war on Iraq may vitiate the war against terrorism.

After the CIA Director, George Tenet, testified to Congress in 2002 about the improbability of Saddam giving weapons of mass destruction to terrorists, the administration continued to repeat the charge as if Tenet hadn't spoken. In February 2003, the White House pressured the unhappy looking Tenet to be a 'team member' and mislead the public by twisting intelligence information to coincide with the Bush thesis. Few believed him when he contradicted the facts of his earlier testimony.

But a letter from dissenting members of the intelligence community stated the conclusion of many expert analysts that 'terrorism is like malaria. You don't eliminate malaria by killing the flies. Rather you must drain the swamp. With an invasion of Iraq, the world can expect to be inundated with swamps breeding terrorists. In human terms, your daughters are unlikely to be able to travel abroad in future years without a large phalanx of security personnel.'[89]

To back up this prediction, the letter sites the CIA reference to a 2002 Gallup poll. The vast majority of 10,000 Muslims in nine countries described the United States as 'ruthless, aggressive, conceited, arrogant, easily provoked and biased.'

We cannot predict the fallout on the Muslim world from a US invasion. But we do have some facts about consequences on US troops from the Gulf War. After a decade plus has lapsed, statistics show that approximately one out of three Gulf War vets returned with undiagnosed disorders of the nervous system. We also know that as Bush has proved generous in his outlays to the military, so too has he been parsimonious with money spent on domestic health, so that Veterans Affairs closed its healthcare system to nearly 200,000 eligible veterans. How will he finance care for the casualties from the impending war?

The public should not fool itself by accepting glibness from White House spinners. P.T. Barnum could have coined the 'Coalition of the Willing' phrase for the suckers. Those 'new European' officials who have taken the bribes don't care about 'disarming Saddam' or 'regime change.' Nor has Bush stated clear goals. They shift with or without the wind. In September 2002, when Saddam readmitted the inspectors, Bush dismissed the move as insufficient. Indeed, Powell scolded the UN Security Council on February 14, 2003, reminding them that 1441 'isn't about inspections—it's about the disarmament of Iraq.' Bush, Rummy, and Condi shout their convenient slogans: disarmament, terrorist connections, regime change and the evil human-rights abusing Saddam himself. Is this the bogus leading the bribed?

During the Gulf War, Bush (41) bribed his coalition in a similar way, warning poor Yemen that their no vote would be the most costly decision they ever made—a total cut-off of US aid.

Despite a few similarities, the difference between the Gulf War, unnecessary as it was, and the impending assault is that Bush (41) had the prudent Powell to advise him to take a conservative path on Iraq. Bush (43), says Gerald Kaufman, former foreign affairs spokesman of Britain's governing Labour Party, 'the most intellectually backward American president of my political lifetime, is surrounded by advisers [including the now imprudent Powell] whose bellicosity is exceeded only by their political, military and diplomatic illiteracy.'[90]

The coalition of the bribed and the warmongering may prevail. History will sneer at them. US taxpayers will finance the war. But the Iraqi civilians will pay the ultimate bill.

YOU CAN'T RUN AN EMPIRE BY REPUBLICAN RULES[*]

Let's stop using the phrase 'international community,' especially as it applies to the United Nations. One member of a civilized community does not tap the phones of other members. But the Bush administration has thrown away the short book of rules that the United States once supposedly applied and has replaced it with a criminal, imperial approach to the United Nations; not with its bullying and intimidating rhetoric during UN Security Council debates over Iraq, but by playing very dirty tricks on delegates from other countries.

---

[*] Originally appeared in *Progreso Weekly*, March 13, 2003, and later *CounterPunch*. On March 2, the *Observer* reported that the National Security Agency had tapped the home and office phones of UN diplomats representing countries on the Security Council.

Since the end of January 2003, the National Security Administration (NSA), the super secret interceptor of worldwide communications, has tapped the office and home phones and e-mails of non-permanent members of UN Security Council delegations in New York. According to an account by Martin Bright, Ed Vulliamy and Peter Beaumont in the March 2, 2003 *Observer*, this 'dirty tricks' operation is part of Washington's 'battle to win votes in favor of war against Iraq.'

The *Observer* reporters refer to a January 31, 2003 memo 'signed by Frank Koza, chief of staff in the "Regional Targets" section of the NSA, which spies on countries that are viewed as strategically important for United States interests.' The memo states that

> The Agency is mounting a surge [an NSA/military term, usually referring to sudden combat or crisis related needs, but increasingly referring to the action items of the day] particularly directed at the UN Security Council [UNSC] members (minus US and GBR of course) for insights as to how the membership is reacting to the on-going debate RE: Iraq, plans to vote on any related resolutions, what related policies/negotiating positions they may be considering, alliances/dependencies, etc—the whole gamut of information that could give US policymakers an edge in obtaining results favorable to US goals or to head off surprises. In RT, that means a QRC [Quick Response Capability, referring to stepping out of routine management rules to get equipment or deploy personnel] surge effort to revive/create efforts against UNSC members Angola, Cameroon, Chile, Bulgaria and Guinea, as well as extra focus on Pakistan UN matters ... whose votes are being fought over by the pro-war party, led by the US and Britain, and the party arguing for more time for UN inspections, led by France, China and Russia.[91]

Koza directs the staff 'to step up its surveillance operations ... to provide up-to-the-minute intelligence for Bush officials on the voting intentions of UN members regarding the issue of Iraq.' The NSA staff is to glean from the illegal eavesdropping 'information that could give US policymakers an edge in obtaining results favorable to US goals or to head off surprises.'

Prior to this revelation, several UN delegates had reported that US officials had threatened their countries with cut-off of aid and other penalties should they vote against the United States. But *Observer* reporters discovered that NSA Adviser Condoleezza Rice, fearful that a defeat at the UN Security Council would create serious domestic political problems in forcing a war against Iraq, decided to go all the way.

Hell, if you can win a US election with hanky-panky, who cares if you use slimy tactics at the UN? Condy's shenanigans reveal that the administration has little concern with maintaining the current international order. So, let's stop talking about international community, rules of the Republic or democracy for that matter.

After the Soviet Union collapsed more than a decade ago, the imperial planners in Washington went to work: how to plot an imperial strategy for the twenty-first century?

Apparently, the consensus document adopted by the Bush (41) and Clinton regimes sustained most of the positions of the late cold war years. The United States would continue to lead an 'alliance' of junior partners in a 'free trade' order: force Third World nations to accept investment on investors' terms. Militarily, the 'new order' meant expanding NATO—who will recall that this military alliance was forged solely to protect the west against Soviet aggression?—while limiting the possibilities of 'rogue states' to assert themselves regionally; also, force them to accept disarmament under treaties that the enforcing nations did not accept for themselves. It was, in short, an extension of historic Wilsonianism, an alliance of the strong 'democracies' forged in 1918–20 in the League of Nations Treaty and extended by Franklin Roosevelt and his successors of both parties.

But two other imperial option papers emerged as well from the policy planners. Indeed, George W. Bush spouted from the 'Pull back because we're overextended' strategy paper in his 2000 campaign. Just as the mainstream consensus strategy opted to keep the United States in its Wilson–Roosevelt mode of alliances, so did Bush revert to Henry Cabot Lodge, Wilson's primary opponent in the 1919–20 debate on the League of Nations.

'The United States is the world's best hope,' Lodge allowed in his November 6, 1919 critique of Wilson's plan to form a world partnership,

> But if you fetter her ... through quarrels of other nations, if you tangle her in the intrigues of Europe, you will destroy her powerful good, and endanger her very existence. Leave her to march freely through the centuries to come, as in the years that have gone. Strong, generous, and confident, she has nobly served mankind. Beware how you trifle with your marvelous inheritance—this great land of ordered liberty. For if we stumble and fall, freedom and civilization everywhere will go down in ruin.[92]

Like the long-dead Lodge, W proposed that the US would run its own empire without tangling itself in European intrigues. He urged a US withdrawal from some of the costly and inefficient international obligations. Speaking like an old-fashioned Republican, W didn't want to involve the country in areas and issues that did not directly pertain to US national interests. The US could still call the shots when it had to, but wouldn't waste its precious capital in what Lodge had once sneered at as 'Balkan wars.' Once it became involved in such remote European messes, Lodge intoned, the US would easily get out.

W got out of several international 'messes' (treaties and agreements) before the Iraq issue arose in its bellicose splendor. He bailed on the Kyoto environmental accords, without even informing his slavish junior partner Tony Blair of England. He ditched the 1972 ABM Treaty, causing much nervous head-shaking in high European and US circles. He ridiculed the International Criminal Court and scrapped even a veneer of objectivity on the Israeli–Palestinian miasma.

Then came 9/11, which set the stage for scrapping the conservative option and adopting the third imperial plan. This 'National Security' policy option called for the United States to assume 'full spectral dominance.' W soon forgot his previous predilection for less involvement and his begrudging accession to the necessity of some involvement, for a shot at the big prize.

Along with an aggressive military thrust throughout the world, setting up bases in at least 62 countries and sending 'advisers' (who really were fighting in places like Colombia) to other countries came the abandonment of the traditional decorum required to deal with both the US's junior partners and the non-essential states (Third World buggers).

Richard Perle and Paul Wolfowitz, Defense Policy Board Chair and Deputy Secretary of Defense respectively, helped craft this new National Security Plan, which calls for an end to even a façade of partnership in the vestigial alliances. The new policy shows muscle—even nuclear muscle—in order to 'pre-empt' all 'potential global competitors,' which means don't let anyone else especially those who might show disobedient tendencies acquire a nuclear weapon.

Another part of this doctrine, to which Perle contributed heavily, calls for Israel to assume an even more important place in the US orbit, raised from 'we'll give you the money and weapons you need' status to that of a regional partner to enforce US order in the midst of unruly Islam.

Even though W and company call themselves conservatives, they have in fact distanced themselves from even the arch conservative Pat Buchanan. In his February 23, 2003 *Los Angeles Times* column, 'Wages of empire,' Buchanan worries about world opinion because 'among Arabs and Turks, the opposition is visceral and well-nigh universal. We are as isolated as the Brits at the time of the Boer War. It is the height of hubris to believe America can indefinitely defy the whole world.' 'Imperialism,' wrote Buchanan, 'is an idea whose time has come and gone and, in any event, we Americans were lousy imperialists.'

Traditional conservatives look for 'exit strategies.' Bush's plan calls for permanent military commitment. Conservatives want to know how the government will pay for the Iraq war and the costs that might logically arise from its aftermath. The acolytes, like the Prez himself, take the 'don't bother me with trivial details' approach, which worries conservatives.

Conservatives remember history, both the world's and the United States'. Even though the President might not have much knowledge of US foreign policy, the well-read Tories can date W's Iraq policies and the radical expansion of US commitments abroad to the historic debate in the US Senate following Woodrow Wilson's presentation to that body for ratification of the League of Nations treaty. While the Wilsonians foresaw a century-long alliance of democratic states in subduing revolution ('outlawing war') and gradually building a viable trading order, the Lodge Republicans opposed the alliance notion and wanted to build a go-it-alone US imperial order.

A third and smaller group of Senators, led by William Borah of Idaho, took a third position. These western state Solons proclaimed incompatible the system of empire and the endurance of principles required to govern a republic. They held the swing votes and helped Lodge defeat the League treaty. Borah's November 19, 1919 words ring with prescient warning.

He said that the League treaty imperils

The underlying, the very first principles of this Republic ... You cannot yoke a government whose fundamental maxim is that of liberty to a government whose first law is that of force and hope to preserve the former. These things are in eternal war, and one must ultimately destroy the other. You may still keep for a time the outward form, you may still delude yourself ... with appearances and symbols, but when you shall have committed this Republic to a scheme of world control based upon the combined military force of the ... great nations of the world, you will have soon destroyed the atmosphere of freedom, of confidence in the self-governing capacity of the masses, in which alone a democracy may thrive. We may become one of the ... dictators of the world, but we shall no longer be master of our own spirit. And what shall it profit us as a Nation if we shall go forth to the domination of the earth ... and lose that fine sense of confidence in the people, the soul of democracy?[93]

Borah's voice occasionally resonated in a Senate speech by Democrats Robert Byrd of West Virginia or Ted Kennedy of Massachusetts. They too warn of the perilous consequences that will result from the imperial course on which W has embarked. But you cannot repeat too often what Borah and the other so-called isolationists said back in 1920: you cannot run an empire by republican rules. The President and his cohorts choose empire over republic with each daily decision, which brings the US and the world closer to catastrophe.

THE THREATS OF EMPIRE—MEXICO, WATCH OUT!*

'We're all Americans,'—the solidarity statement of French President Jacques Chirac after 9/11.

'If you're really Americans, you better do what I say or else!'—George W. Bush, rehearsing before his Press Seance on March 5, 2003.

'Any country that doesn't go along with us will be paying a very heavy price.'

This warning to Mexican officials suggesting that they should not vote against the US–Great Britain sponsored war resolution in the Security Council came from an unnamed US diplomat. The White House ordered US officials to go directly to the capitals of UN Security Council member states to issue these 'warnings.'

Immediately after the 9/11 events, much of the world, including long-time adversaries like Fidel Castro, offered messages of solidarity. 'Nous sommes Américains,' President Chirac said, summing up the feelings of most Europeans. Over the subsequent year and a half, George W. Bush, as spokesman for a small group of imperial zealots, has more than reversed that positive sentiment. Indeed, he may have interpreted the pro-American sentiment as meaning that the rest of the world would now obey his orders, especially around the issue of waging war against Iraq—which he mystically links, since he has no evidence, to the 9/11 tragedy.

The world has responded to Bush's bullying approach with fear and loathing. Most of the world fears the United States. Pollsters regularly report that Europeans, Asians, Africans and Latin Americans think that the United States—not Iraq or North Korea—constitutes the greatest threat to peace.

It has become apparent as a result of US maneuvering to entice the UN Security Council to support Bush's war that Washington will use whatever it deems necessary to force the UN body into the façade of an agreement.

The tactics to reach consensus over the last months may have set new levels for international bribery, blatant coercion and public prevarication, but the methods themselves date back to other US imperial plans. Washington has become addicted to running the world and to using other

---

* Appeared in *CounterPunch*, March 22, 2003, and *Progreso Weekly*. In the corridors of the UN, US diplomats leveled heavy threats to representatives of other countries. Vote our way or else!

governments to accomplish its ends: to make the nations of the world obedient to US policy demands, however they may fluctuate.

Over the last 50 years, the CIA used covert operations to overthrow disobedient governments in Iran, Guatemala, Brazil, Chile and Nicaragua. That's the short list. It invaded dozens of others to remove governments or government leaders. In the 1980s alone, Washington practiced serial intervention in Central America, invaded Grenada and 'arrested' General Noriega in Panama. In addition, the United States has routinely bribed and intimidated other governments to 'cooperate' in its covert schemes and dirty tricks.

Mexican government officials should take heed of newly declassified documents that reveal that from 1964 on the Johnson administration used Mexico as a source to harass and spy on Cuba. The spying continued into the 1970s under Nixon.

On March 2, 2003, the Mexican *Proceso* magazine published some of the hitherto secret papers obtained by Kate Doyle of the National Security Archives. The documents should not only embarrass those Mexican officials who connived with the CIA back then, but serve as an admonition to President Fox as well.

Under President Gustavo Diaz Ordaz (1964–70) and his successor, Luis Echeverria Alvarez (1970–76), the Mexican government cooperated with Washington to harass persons traveling to Cuba. The Mexicans imposed one condition, however: Washington would publicly accept the veneer of Mexico's independent status regarding Cuba and recognize Mexico's sovereign right to maintain relations with Cuba. Washington readily agreed and from then on only pretended annoyance at Mexico for retaining her ties to Cuba. Meanwhile, the CIA used Mexican territory and its government officials for dirty tricks.

In addition to the documents, the Archives obtained transcripts of President Lyndon Johnson's taped phone conversations, which extended the CIA's espionage field into Cuba itself. Indeed, as Susan Ferriss writes in the March 6, 2003 *Palm Beach Post*, 'Johnson struck a secret deal with Mexico in 1964 that converted at least some of Mexico's diplomats in Cuba into Our Men in Havana—spies who passed information about the island and its Soviet allies directly to the White House.'

By July 1964, the United States had twisted every other government arm in Latin America to force them to vote to expel Cuba from the OAS and almost every other regional organization, but also to break all relations with the communist island. The CIA plotters, however, encouraged Mexican officials to parade their supposed 'rejection' of Washington pressure and show the world how solidly independent they were. Indeed, shortly after his inauguration, Mexico's new President proclaimed his everlasting friendship with Cuba's Fidel Castro. Yes, with friends like Diaz Ordaz ...

Internally, Mexico used its alleged pro-Cuba stance to offset its repressive policies against its own left. As Mexican police and army units tortured and murdered revolutionaries throughout the country, presidents Diaz Ordaz and Echeverria held up the Cuba card to show their international 'revolutionary' commitment.

In 1967 I went to Mexico to transfer to the Cubana flight to Havana to film a public television documentary. I witnessed some of these CIA shenanigans. First, the Mexicans forced Cuba-bound travelers from the United States who wished to return through Mexico to obtain permission from the Gobernacion Ministry (Interior).

Mexico required that the traveler possess official US State Department permission to travel. Then, the process began, which took a couple of days and cost—in bribes—about 100 pesos (about $30 in those days). After checking in at the Cubana counter at the Mexico City airport (the only air route to Cuba in the hemisphere), members of the film crew and I were whisked to a special room. There, uniformed Mexican officials demanded that we pose for photographs, as we held numbers over our chests. Following that, we moved to the next obstacle. A man wearing a Mexican immigration police uniform typed on an ancient Underwood our answers to a six-page questionnaire, probing into the personal and political affairs of each individual. I asked the official why he did this and under whose orders he operated. Instead of answering he threatened: 'Answer my questions or we shall deport you.'

When the CIA agents, dressed as Mexican officials, had finished photographing and interrogating the passengers, other uniformed officials shepherded the travelers to the farthest point of the airport, about a half-a-mile walk with carry-on bags. Then we boarded the oven-like Soviet-built Cubana plane, which apparently did not get permission to use the cool air pump used by other commercial aircraft. What seemed like eons later, yet another uniformed official 'inspected' the plane and when the heat appeared to get to him he gave the nod to take off. Needless to say, the passengers cheered as the plane took off.

I underwent this experience twice more in 1968 and again in 1969 on subsequent film expeditions. Once in Cuba, I had to get the Gobernacion document validated by the Mexican consulate in Havana (another bribe). Failure to do this meant one had to return to the United States via Madrid or Prague.

The new documents shed more light on CIA operations previously aired by Philip Agee. A CIA official who resigned and told all, Agee estimated that 'the [Mexico CIA] station's annual budget even then was $5,500,000. And the Mexicans were very cooperative. With Mexican security's help, the station was able to tap as many as 40 telephone lines at once. The president of the country at the time, Diaz Ordaz, was a very close CIA collaborator. So was his predecessor.'[94] In his August 1975 *Playboy* interview, Agee claimed that 'Mexican president, Luis Echeverria also was a station contact—when he was Diaz Ordaz' minister for internal security.'

In 1969, Fidel Castro revealed to me yet another CIA ploy. The Cuban government had purchased from a Mexican company a hydraulically-operated sugar cane cutting machine. This cutter had the ability to cut the cane at the right place on the stalk even on uneven terrain. When Cuban technicians assembled the machine, however, it immediately malfunctioned. Referring to the accompanying instruction manual, they found gibberish in place of real repair instructions. Edward Lamb, the factory's owner, investigated the problem and discovered that the CIA had sabotaged the machine and rewritten the instruction manual, with the cooperation of Mexican authorities.

Similarly, in the early 1970s, the CIA poisoned a batch of pineapple seedlings Cuba had purchased from a Mexican enterprise so that, when they arrived in Cuba, the baby pineapple plants had all died.

Under Nixon, the CIA operations became downright gangster-like in their texture. In 1970, a young Cuba-bound American woman told me of her adventure. She and five other anti-war activists arrived at the Mexico City airport where Mexican CIA agents, flashing phony badges and real guns, kidnapped them. The armed agents placed them in two cars with locked rear doors and drove them non-stop—except for bathroom breaks—to the US border. Once there, US immigration authorities, expecting the delivery, took the six and told them to go home.

These few examples of thousands constitute illegal interference in routine commercial and travel relations between Cuba and Mexico. They could not have transpired without the active complicity of the Mexican government. In its 70-year-long rule, the PRI Party clung to the myth that it represented the spirit of the revolution of 1910 that aimed at overthrowing the ruling corrupt clique. In fact, as the new documents show, Washington found it relatively easy to bribe and intimidate Mexico's top officials.

Now, Mexico occupies a strategic seat as one of ten non-permanent members of the UN Security Council. Once again, US officials revert to their successful tactics of the past: bribes and intimidation. They even trotted out Henry Kissinger, a world-class intimidator, to warn Mexico of the consequences of opposition to the US war position.

But conditions have changed. Mexican voters ended the seven decades of PRI rule in 2000 when they chose Vicente Fox of the PAN party as their new chief executive officer. As Mexico has democratized slowly over the years, public opinion now carries some weight.

Fox has not delivered on his promises. Indeed, he has vacillated and reneged on key pledges, like delivering a treaty with Washington to legalize more than three million Mexicans living in the United States. He has also discovered that no amount of servility has induced Washington to concede on even minimal issues. In Mexico's political cartoon world, Fox has earned a brown nose for his avid butt-kissing. Now Mexico's UN delegate on the Security Council must vote with or against the United States. Washington, as always, says: 'Vote our way, or else!' Mexican public opinion polls indicate that almost 80 per cent or more of the adult population oppose US war policies with Iraq.

Unlike the 1960s, when Johnson allowed Mexico to maintain its façade of independence, the 2003 US policies brook not even a thin covering of disobedience. In his unrelenting pursuit of war with Iraq, Bush demands that President Fox and the other heads of state from the UN Security Council members betray the wishes of their own people, who have manifested decisive anti-war sentiments. Like some of his predecessors, Bush does not think twice about altering the fate of millions of people in the world. He did take seriously the sentiment after 9/11. He understood what it meant when the French said: 'We are all Americans.' Now he has added to that understanding: 'Since you admit to being Americans, you better do what I say!'

TECHNOLOGICAL MASSACRE IN IRAQ ALSO LEAVES THE UN IN CRITICAL CONDITION[*]

'We must make clear to the Germans that the wrong for which their fallen leaders are on trial is not that they lost the war, but that they started it. And we must not allow ourselves to be drawn into a trial of the causes of the war, for our position is that no grievances or policies will justify resort to aggressive war. It is utterly renounced and condemned as an instrument of policy.'—Supreme Court Justice Robert L. Jackson, US Representative to the International Conference on Military Trials, August 12, 1945[95]

---

[*]   Appeared in *CounterPunch*, March 28, 2003, and *Progreso Weekly*. The US-led Coalition bombing of Iraq began on March 19 with what White House officials called a 'decapitation attack.'

Bombs rained on Baghdad. Buildings I had visited in September 2002 had disappeared in fire and smoke. I hoped that the smiling Iraqi janitors and maintenance staff who had said 'Welcome' in heavily accented English had not remained on the premises. In Tariq Aziz's office, now obliterated, the Deputy Prime Minister resisted former senator Jim Abourezk and Congressman Nick Rahall's persuasive arguments to allow the UN weapons inspectors to return to Iraq. 'Without guarantees that he [Bush] will not attack, why should we concede?' he asked. The inspectors, after all, had given President Clinton the coordinates for targets to bomb and had provided US and British intelligence with data on military matters far a field from weapons of mass destruction. 'We're doomed if we do [let the inspectors in] and doomed if we don't,' said Aziz, 'you better don't.' Iraqi leaders overruled him and the inspectors returned. I don't know if they will find evidence of the much touted hidden weapons, but Aziz has proven correct.

The 'liberation of Iraq,' announced the President on March 19, was underway. I watched the improved rerun of the TV light show of bombs and missiles destroying property, followed by truly shocking and awesome shots of flames and smoke, while an embedded voice prattled on with details of the coalition's progress. The 103rd captured blah blah, while the 74th marched northward with little opposition. Corporal Smith of the 3rd infantry wrote a letter to his wife, while Private Jones talked with tears in his eyes about his newborn baby girl.

A few Marine casualties, no reports of the numbers of Iraqi dead, some speculation as to the number of Iraqis who had surrendered, rumors of Saddam being dead or wounded. Then, some war footage of US technology obliterating the primitive Iraqi forces. Yes, truth becomes war's first victim. Indeed, it had suffered near fatal wounds before the war. But how do we separate the big lies from the innocuous ones?

The lies about how many dead and wounded, how many Iraqis surrendered and in which direction the 104th was moving pale in comparison with the foundation of lies established before the technological massacre began. In December 2002, the White House declared that 'the greatest danger our nation faces lies at the crossroads of radicalism and technology.' As David von Drehle quoted a security document in the March 21, 2003 *Washington Post*, 'Our enemies have openly declared that they are seeking weapons of mass destruction ... The United States will not allow these efforts to succeed.'

Instead of using verbal logic, Washington now relies on the logic of bombing, the 'shock and awe' method of reasoning. It has invented a cause: dethroning tyrants, liberating oppressed people and assuring the American people that their enemies or potential enemies do not possess weapons of mass destruction that they can use or deliver to terrorists.

The United States doesn't have a monopoly on weapons of mass destruction but it can certainly out-compete the rest of the world combined as it has demonstrated over the last dozen years in the 1991 Gulf War and in serial bombings of various Third World targets since then. No matter how short or warped memories have become, surely someone will recall that the United States is unique among nations for its use of atomic weapons, that the United States and England engaged in firebombing entire cities in Germany and Japan, that the United States has just tested a MOAB (mother of all bombs) and remains the only nation that has threatened to use nuclear weapons in pre-emptive strikes against nations it defines as potential threats. Britain, by the way, introduced poison gas as a weapon in the Middle East after World War I to suppress nationalist uprisings.

One of Bush's most pernicious lies ties the bin Laden terrorists to Saddam Hussein. In his speeches and press conferences, he had repeated references to Iraq and the 9/11 ghouls so often that, according to polls, nearly half the US public believed such ties actually existed. I wonder why he doesn't show us or our skeptical allies some solid evidence of these connections?

In my fantasy I see a day when courageous editors fashion headlines or TV teases: 'Bush repeats same old crap!' Instead, they uncritically repeat his lies and then cut to the next unrelated story or commercial. Similarly, when the administration used forged documents to try to show that Saddam had an ongoing nuclear program, the media showed no skepticism. After the war began, however, the following appeared.

'On the eve of Mr. Bush's ultimatum, it came to light that a key piece of evidence used by the Bush administration to link Iraq to a nuclear weapons program is a forgery,' wrote the conservative Craig Paul Roberts in the March 21, 2003 *Washington Times*. Roberts reports that Senator Jay Rockefeller of West Virginia, the ranking Democrat on the Senate Intelligence Committee, has asked the FBI to investigate the origin of the forged documents that the Bush administration used to make its case that Saddam Hussein possesses weapons of mass destruction. The Secretary of State, Colin Powell, denies that the Bush administration created the phony documents. 'It came from other sources,' Mr. Powell told Congress, but he could not identify the source.

On March 22, after the bombs had destroyed Baghdad, *Washington Post* reporters Dana Priest and Karen DeYoung wrote that CIA officials now say they communicated significant doubts to the administration about the evidence backing up charges that Iraq tried to purchase uranium from Africa for nuclear weapons, charges that found their way into President Bush's State of the Union address, a State Department 'fact sheet' and public remarks by numerous senior officials.

According to several officials, decisions about what information to declassify and use to make the administration's public case have been made by a small group that includes top CIA and National Security Council officials. 'The policy guys make decisions about things like this,' said one official, referring to the uranium evidence. When the State Department 'fact sheet' was issued, the official said, 'people winced and thought, "Why are you repeating this trash?"'[96]

But these officials didn't resign and the media does not emphasize the administration's duplicity. Indeed, Fox and CNN reporters continued to repeat lies about Saddam's nuclear program and underplayed the revelation about the forged documents. Lies become headlines. Truth screams silently in pain!

Baby Bush launched his war or Technological Massacre II to 'disarm Iraq,' or 'strike a blow against terrorism,' or carry out 'regime change' or 'bring democracy' or avenge his father, or get the oil, or please the Israelis— depending on which day you asked. Using massive quantities of weapons of mass destruction to level a city of 5 million people, the US armed forces will now seek out Saddam's tiny—if existent—quantity of biological and chemical weapons. I have every reason to believe they will find it whether or not Saddam really had it.

A few journalists might raise skeptical questions, but most will accept whatever proof Bush offers to justify his first vicarious taste of combat, which he continues to speak with several tongues. The 'shock and awe' display will of course intimidate dictators who harbor terrorists and direct non-harborers in the region toward democracy.

The elated Iraqi people will now build a free society. This means, I suppose, that they will now join the corporate global order as proper factory workers and consumers. People of Iran, North Korea, Libya, Cuba etc. take note!

Iraq will soon shine as an example of freedom to all other Islamic societies, the President has promised. Above all, the massive tonnage dropped on Iraq should signal to the entire world: don't mess with the United States of America. Ironically, of course, Iraq did not provoke the United States or threaten it directly or indirectly. That little fact no longer matters. The victors don't need to worry about facing war crimes tribunals yet.

In the past two years, the always vague meaning of 'national security' has changed again. 'The struggle against global terrorism is different from any other war in our history,' wrote the authors of the September 2002 National Security doctrine paper.[97] The paper warned that the war against the elusive enemy will be fought on many fronts and over an extended period of time.

So if you've still retained a modicum of human sensibility, don't expect your feelings of horror to abate. The authors of the new doctrine declare that 'progress will come through the persistent accumulation of successes some seen, some unseen.' Remember the words of Bush to Congress on September 20, 2001: 'Americans should not expect one battle, but a lengthy campaign unlike any other we have ever seen,' Bush declared. 'The American people need to know we're facing a different enemy than we have ever faced. The United States of America will use all our resources to conquer this enemy.'

Bush targeted not just terrorists but also sovereign nations that 'harbor' terrorists. And the mission continued to expand. By September 2002, a year after the attacks, the new security strategy cast the net broadly, declaring that 'America will hold to account nations that are compromised by terror.' He has yet to define 'compromised.'

The overreaching strategy behind the 'shock and awe' bombing of Baghdad aims at the masses of Middle Eastern people who now hate America more than ever.

As Joe Stalin purportedly asked after an adviser told him of the Pope's opposition to his policies, 'how many divisions does the Pope have?' We shall soon find out how many divisions the Arab streets have, how many world public opinion can wield and how many the anti-war protestors inside the United States and the United Kingdom can put into play. Divisions can boycott US products and make life seriously uncomfortable for US and British business travelers, emissaries and tourists. This is democracy.

When the President speaks of democracy he means its opposite whether or not he knows enough to acknowledge it. With his beady eyes rolling in reverie, Bush praises the virtues of democracy as if oblivious to the fact that he consorts with anti-democratic tyrants in a host of countries, like Pakistan, Kazakhstan and Kuwait. He talks of spreading freedom and liberty abroad while Attorney General Ayatollah Ashcroft reduces domestic liberties in the US.

If that's not enough, prepare for a world in which the authors of the war will try to kill the United Nations or reduce it to the benign status of the League of Nations before World War II. If you doubt this, see Richard Perle's column, reprinted in the March 21, 2003 *Guardian*. The headline reads: 'Thank God for the death of the UN.'

In 1964, Mario Savio exhorted students at the Berkeley Free Speech Movement. His words remain the appropriate response to the Perles and the imperialists in the White House.

There is a time when the operation of the machine becomes so odious, makes you so sick at heart, that you can't take part; and you've got to put your bodies upon the gears and upon the wheels, upon the levers, upon all the apparatus and you've got to make it stop.[98]

IRAQ WAR: A POLICY OF CHRISTIAN AND JEWISH FUNDAMENTALISM; WORSE LIES AHEAD*

'Wars are poor chisels for carving out peaceful tomorrows.—Martin Luther King Jr.[99]

Congratulations to George W. Bush, winner and still champion after defeating a highly ranked heavyweight contender! Indeed, the heroic US victory in Iraq should engrave 43's name in the history books. The Bush Doctrine means fighting 'pre-emptive' wars with disarmed nations that in the very distant future might conceivably threaten US interests. In Christian lore, the US invasion of Iraq will find its justification in the first three words of the adage: 'Do unto others.'

The biblical talk overflowed from the White House, but military commanders, under orders from their civilian bosses, dispatched troops to protect the oilfields while other US soldiers, also under orders, stood by and allowed if not encouraged the destruction of the very sacred relics to which the Bible refers. 'Praise God and speak reverently of His works, but watch carefully over your newly acquired treasure,' the Bible should have said.

The gap between words and deeds should make people laugh as we already hear threats of the next war. Those who screamed loudest in Congress about supporting US troops cut their benefits. No matter! The headlines and lead stories barely reported that. Instead, we saw on TV the American flag—flying high and being waved, of course. A good section of the anxious US public seems eager to accept as truth any nonsense uttered from the White House and repeated in the media. Use God early and often in each speech!

'Let the word go forth,' George Bush has chosen war as his (or His) method of forging peace—and getting re-elected. Taking his orders from his own special Christian God and his brilliant political manipulators, Bush has set out on a divine mission of 'liberation.' The billion people who adhere to the Islamic faith—do they share a collective memory of the Crusades?—should feel rightfully apprehensive.

With the bodies of Iraqis still unburied and the once fabled ancient treasures either missing or destroyed, the Defense Secretary, Rumsfeld, threatens Syria. Nothing new! It's the old 'possessing weapons of mass destruction' and 'harboring terrorists' crap. Syrians should understand that

---

* Originally appeared in *Progreso Weekly*, April 26, 2003 and *CounterPunch*. Yes, the Iraqis stop shooting and critical members of the media reveal the strange union between anti-Semitic Christian fundamentalists and neo-conservative Jews. In this sexless power marriage, the rest of us get fucked.

the President makes rapid decisions. He needs no evidence to convince him of the righteous course. He acts with an air of total confidence. Policy depends not on facts or analysis, but on his trusted gut feeling about good and evil. He explained to an Oklahoma City audience what distinguishes 'us' from 'them.'

On August 29, 2002, he said: 'See, we love—we love freedom. That's what they didn't understand. They hate things; we love things. They act out of hatred; we don't seek revenge, we seek justice out of love.'[100]

To combat evil, to find justice and love, the best of human nature, Bush of course relies on war—to obtain peace. And God, for Bush, made us the most powerful military force. So, as soon as US forces were ready for action after 9/11, Bush ordered them to attack the mighty Taliban in Afghanistan. When the bombs and missiles exploded, the Afghan losses made the numbers lost in the World Trade Center and the Pentagon pale. Explosives rained on the land ruled by the Saudi-backed fundamentalists where wicked Al-Qaeda had training camps.

Few of the cognoscenti saw Afghanistan as the beginning of a new US imperial order. Whatever Bush said, they took it as logical 'revenge.' Surely, the Republican dominated ruling elite would temper 'the youngster's' overseas behavior. But the young emperor, using terrorism as his loose metaphor for all evil, continued to pursue war in the evil region—against Iraq. Bush made it clear to other governments that he cared not a Texas hoot what they think.

Wow, says Hans Blix, the former chief UN weapons inspector. On April 9, 2003, Blix told *El Pais* in Madrid that 'there is evidence that this war was planned well in advance. Sometimes this raises doubts about their attitude to the (weapons) inspections.' Was Blix naïve?

Perhaps he didn't take Bush's threats seriously because they rang with that religious fundamentalist timbre that seemed, well, inappropriate for modern, sophisticated US power. But Bush had made his intentions clear. On September 5, 2002, Bush spoke to Iraq, Syria, Iran, Libya and others using a Louisville, Kentucky audience as his medium: 'I want to send the signal to our enemy that you have aroused a compassionate and decent and mighty nation, and we're going to hunt you down.'

A war to bring about his deepest religious desires! 'You need to tell your loved ones, the little ones in particular, that when they hear the President talking about Al-Qaeda, Iraq and other places, I do so because I long for peace.'

For Bush—ignorant of Orwell's *Nineteen Eighty-Four*—peace meant war. 'When we need to be plenty tough, we're going to be plenty tough. And they're [the terrorists] learning another thing about America. When we need to be compassionate and loving, we can be compassionate and loving, too.'

Most pundits and politicians apparently missed the sea change in world affairs that resulted from the 9/11 events. What many saw as a temporary shift – the revenge cycle—has turned into a long-term alteration in the geopolitical order. 9/11 served as a US equivalent of Hitler's 1933 Reichstag fire in which 'fighting terrorism' became the pretext for radical new forms of control at home and abroad.

Look at the changes. In place of law, the UN, NATO and other treaties, Bush substituted naked US power, which he and his minions justify either with Biblical jibberish or neo-Metternichean jargon. (Prince Klemens von Metternich led Austria on its imperial path during the first half of the nineteenth century. Metternich stressed that heads of state must make policies including war to secure peace. He saw revolution and rebellious or non-complaint behavior as diseases and tried to suppress them everywhere.)

To wage war, Bush needed sufficient backing at home—to Hell with the rest of the world. So, he used the tried and true demonization method, insinuating that the devilish Saddam had somehow directed the 9/11 attacks. In his speeches and press conferences, he demonized a truly bad man without presenting any evidence of actual links that Saddam had to terrorists or weapons of mass destruction. These same accusatory speeches came replete with multiple references to God and peace.

The spin worked. By March 19, 2003, when US forces invaded Iraq, a substantial percentage of the US public had become convinced that Saddam had not only 'gassed his own people' but had inflicted the 9/11 damage on 'us.' Thus, Bush was right to invade.

Most of the US's allies—except for Britain, Spain and Australia—had watched with an air of disbelief the belligerent foreplay before the aggressive penetration. Bush really wouldn't make war without Security Council backing! Then, when he made war, they protested and wrung their hands.

They had expected the civilized Colin Powell to stall the war machine. After all, important sectors of the ruling elite, including Daddy Bush (41) and his *consigliere* James Baker and Brent Scowcroft had evinced serious reservations about going ahead without UN support.

But the supposedly prudent Secretary of State demonstrated that his servility outweighed his caution. When the crucial debate occurred in the United Nations Security Council, the opponents of war had insufficient *cojones* to stand dramatically against Bush's war of naked, unprovoked aggression. Nor did the leading Democrats—there were a few exceptions like the Democrats Senator Robert Byrd from West Virginia and Congressman Dennis Kucinich from Ohio—have the courage to warn him and the nefarious chicken hawks who planned the attack that they were about to commit war crimes.

The Bushies laughed at the wussy-like Democrats, scoffed at the weak-willed European opposition, sneered at the once-powerful Russians and commercially addicted Chinese. They occasionally patted Blair, America's pet poodle, on the head and scorned those Cassandras who warned about the reaction of 'the angry Arab street' and 'world public opinion.'

'How many divisions do they have?' Bush might well have asked, paraphrasing Stalin's mocking of the Pope who disapproved of his policies as his administration practiced the politics of raw power.

They took what had been peripheral issues at best—like Iraq having weapons of mass destruction and links to Al-Qaeda as imminent threats to US security—and made them central. Simultaneously, they deftly distorted facts that the media predictably lacked the curiosity to check. But they knew they could count on the media to present memory-eroding volleys of changing 'Reality TV in Iraq' images.

When the ruling elite leaned on Bush to get UN backing before going to war, the Bushies took spinning to a new level. Saddam, they charged, had violated UN Security Council resolutions. The very organization that Bush had routinely disparaged as worthless, now took on holy status. Saddam's sin of sins was his violation of UN resolutions.

So, repetition of charges: weapons of mass destruction, links to Al-Qaeda, violation of UN resolutions and 'he tried to kill Daddy'—referring to an ambiguous assassination attempt in Kuwait in 1993—became the administration mantra. At no time did the President present evidence. He simply repeated the accusations. Hey, who are you going to believe, your president or the guy who gassed his own people?

Instead of telling him to 'go sleep it off,' the cowardly Democrats, ever fearful that someone will expose them as 'weak,' wrung their hands, publicly accepted Bush's claptrap and in October 2002 awarded him special wartime powers (the Senate vote was 77–23).

The Bush planners had already decided to fight this war without concern for law (a fig leaf at best) or international opinion. It surprised few people that the immense superiority of US weaponry defeated a far weaker military force—especially one like Iraq's, which had basically disarmed before the invasion. The Americans didn't even really need the British.

The lesson: circumvent international law, the UN and world public opinion and substitute brute force and the world will grasp the essentials of the US order in the twenty-first century. Hail America, America waives the rules!

Of course, it helped to target a universally despised villain and fool. But Saddam didn't use mass destruction weapons against the invading

Americans and British. Perhaps he didn't have any such lethal arms. Time will tell.

The historical record shows US administrations in the 1970s and 1980s cooperating with this ogre when it suited their interests. Documents show the Defense Secretary, Donald Rumsfeld, shaking Saddam's hand in 1983 as President Reagan's envoy. Rummy helped facilitate Iraq's acquisition of chemical and biological weapons and US logistical help to deploy them.

Coincidentally, several administration officials have close ties to companies that will materially benefit from the war, like the Vice President, Cheney, former CEO of Halliburton that will make billions on the rebuilding of Iraq. In the March 17, 2003 *New Yorker*, Seymour Hersh offers substantial evidence to show that US Defense Policy Board Chairman, Richard Perle, used his inside position to charge substantial fees. No reason not to do well while doing good!

These Jewish neo-cons and Christian fundamentalists have made a marriage of bellicose convenience, in which the rest of the world gets screwed. They see the world as theirs to win—unless something untoward occurs in the 2004 election or the economy continues its downward spiral.

Consequences? Bush hasn't talked about them. He dismissed the appearance of up to 20 million people demonstrating in the streets of cities throughout the world as comparable to a 'focus group.'[101]

But, as Seumas Milne reports,[102] the North Koreans are paying close attention to both Bush's policies and the reaction to them. 'As anti-war and anti-American demonstrations erupt throughout the world,' he writes, 'North Korea's foreign ministry dramatized one sobering lesson drawn from this four week war.'

A North Korean government official said: '"The Iraqi war shows that to allow disarmament through inspections does not help avert a war, but rather sparks it."' The North Koreans concluded that to prevent attacks on nations the United States has placed in the axis of evil, requires "a tremendous military deterrent force."'

As the sounds of prayer emanate from the White House, Milne sees the chicken hawk planners of the Iraq war circling 'around Syria and Iran.' They have provided 'a powerful boost to nuclear proliferation.' He concludes that 'anti-western terror attacks seem inevitable, offset only by the likelihood of a growing international mobilization against the new messianic imperialism.'

Amen, I say, in my non-religious way. I, like tens of millions of others, will continue to resist.

FINAL THOUGHTS:
Stop Shopping, Looking in the Mirror and Worrying About Your Spare Tires and Cellulite and Make Your Own History

'Pettiness separates. Breadth unites. Let us be broad and big. Let us not overlook vital things because of the bulk of trifles confronting us.'—Emma Goldman, briefly banned in Berkeley CA, January 2003[103]

One of my daughters regrets not having lived in the 1960s. Why? I naively ask.

'Duh!' she replies. 'Sex, drugs and rock 'n' roll, Dad. And people did meaningful politics.'

Yes, in that era millions of young people—myself included—demonstrated, sat in, burned draft cards, occupied selective service centers, put our bodies on the line for desegregation and to stop the unjust war against the Vietnamese people. Millions of people also had a vision of a more equal and just society. The sixties generation had a culture that included vigorous and anarchic dancing, using mind enhancing or hallucinatory drugs and spending weekends at concerts with hundreds of thousands of others.

Out of the 1960s came desegregation, movements for women's equality, gay rights, black and Chicano rights, environmental militancy and movements that today even the Republican Senator Trent Lott from Mississippi is forced to accept—at least publicly—as correct and just.

After the 1960s and early 1970s, the spirit that gave rise to the various liberation movements continued but culturally gave way to consumption as the overriding national ethos. Americans received a barrage of ever more messages to purchase ever more commodities and services to relieve their ever greater inadequacies and anxieties.

Under the first layer of urgent messages lay a more important underlying message. The 'buy or else' message contained its own ethic; well, code if you like. It forced the receiver of the message to internalize a set of priorities, the first of which was to understand that his or her own gratification had become the most important and immediate issue in the world. The new messages switched the actor's focus. From 'Ho, Ho, Ho Chi Minh, the NLF is going to win'[104] or the other slogans of the 1960s that showed how the anti-war demonstrators understood themselves as historical actors, members of a historical force, the new assault on the brain, focused on consumers, individuals who became what Walter Benjamin quipped 'seduced by the sex appeal of the inorganic.'[105]

Unlike the Beatles' lesson of the 1960s, the Ronald Reagan ethos taught that 'money can buy you love.' The meaning of culture itself changed.

'When I think of culture,' one of Barbara Kruger's art works proclaims, 'I take out my checkbook.'

Instead of making history in the streets, 'you make history when you do business,' Kruger sarcastically concludes. She encapsulates the consumer ethic: 'Buy me. I'll change your life.'

Instead of life gaining meaning by participation in the larger world of events, the advertiser tells you that it acquires real significance from the purchase of things. What was described as the spiritual emptiness of the 1980s and 1990s, that malaise of soul that comes with ownership of things, meant that Americans turned inward—away from history making. Those that felt unfulfilled were exhorted to buy more, shop more fervently. They had to accept the notion that their emotional well-being had become addictively tied to the purchase of healing commodities.

This change of cultural values for young and educated people entered the university curriculum as well. Marketing majors abounded, as business schools proliferated. Education itself took on the stripes of training for business careers. Business class, business travel, business values and standards, even business ethics became phrases of the late twentieth century. 'The empty phrase,' wrote Benjamin, 'is the label that makes a thought marketable.'[106]

With the help of the new ad industry, merchandise acquired sex appeal so as better to 'market' it. Those who could not get into sync with the new ethos found themselves in lonely exile in their own country, sinking 'into the mire of common sense,' as Julia Kristeva noted.[107]

In my periodic sojourns to the barbershop, now pretentiously known as the hair styling emporium, I listen to the ordinariness of AM radio music and the endless chatter about hairdos, male and female. I begged once to listen to one of the presidential debates and the assistant manager looked at me as if I had just recently arrived from Timbuktu. 'What has politics got to do with anything?' she asked, shaking her head with a certainty that I dared not challenge.

'Music is the best way to kill time,' my hair stylist confided. Yes, killing time and styling hair, what a way to live until one dies!

But the dumbing down and dulling of sensibilities cannot endure. The average adult American receives 3,000 plus urgent commercial messages a day. Few if any of them relate to human needs or teach meaningful lessons. This inundation of trivia may have dampened the embers of the human spirit. It almost certainly has clogged the brain's natural filtration process. But the limits of shopping as the basis for imperial culture have become obvious to many millions. And people have begun to return to the streets to protest against the war with Iraq. On campuses, students have turned their attention to war, sweat shops, to unjust wages and worsening conditions for janitors and service workers on campus.

The memories of the 1960s, the stories told by those who lived through those years and recall how fully realized they felt—albeit frustrated at their inability to change things quickly—have begun to filter down to the youth of today. It's not sex, now more dangerous than in the sixties, drugs, no longer so novel, or rock 'n' roll, musically duller without the Beatles and young Stones, that lures people into political activity or even accompanies it. A new spirit of solidarity has developed, discovered by those who marched and demonstrated against the unfair world order in Seattle, Washington DC and other places and then took to the streets, joined by millions more, to protest against the war against Iraq.

The resistance to the new world order erupted symbolically and actually on January 1, 1994. Mayan Indians took over eight municipalities in Mexico's south-eastern state of Chiapas. The Zapatista Army of National Liberation demanded more than land and justice. They called for genuine democracy, not routine electionism. They called for the inclusion of indigenous people in world politics, from which they had been excluded. They called also for a cultural and political war against neo-liberalism, the model that would destroy old cultures and focus human energy on producing, distributing, advertising, marketing and shopping.

Hey, I tell my students, you have only one shot at living—unless you believe in reincarnation. You can spend your time working toward buying the Maserati and on your deathbed regret that you never got it. Or, you can become an actor in your world, in your time and join other participants whose efforts have brought about some victories for justice and equality.

Notes

1. On October 4, 2001, the first United States post-9/11 anthrax outbreak was reported after a worker at the Boca Raton, Florida based American Media tabloid newspaper publisher died from inhalation of anthrax. After a third worker tested positive, on October 11 the FBI launched a criminal investigation into the anthrax outbreak at American Media. Later that month, NBC anchor Tom Brokaw and South Dakota Democratic Senator Tom Daschle both received anthrax-laced letters.
2. Cited in the California Governor Gray Davis' January 9, 2003 State of the State address. Available online at <http://www.democraticgovernors.org/sos2003/california.html>
3. James Flanigan, 'China's import needs make it as much an opportunity as a threat,' *Los Angeles Times*, December 22, 2002.
4. 'Statement by the President on tax agreement,' May 1, 2001. Available online at <http://www.whitehouse.gov/news/releases/2001/05/20010501–9.html>
5. In Bush's September 20, 2001 address to Congress, he said, 'They [the terrorists] hate our freedoms—our freedom of religion, our freedom of speech, our freedom to vote and assemble and disagree with each other.' See text of full address online at <http://www.whitehouse.gov/news/releases/2001/09/20010920–8.html>
6. Friedman, HarperCollins, 1999.
7. Medici's remark is much quoted and attributed to many authors, among them Gordon Laxer from the University of Alberta, 'What's an economy for?,' *The Post (A Publication of the Parkland Institute)*, Vol. 1, No. 2, Fall 1997.
8. The Erhard Seminars Training mass-therapy program of self-improvement was founded by Werner Erhard in 1971. EST offered intense courses designed to 'rewire' people's consciousness. Thousands of well-educated people fell for this 'make yourself feel good, confident and powerful' gibberish during the 1970s.
9. Gore, Plume, 1993.
10. Dowd, 'The unelection day,' *New York Times*, November 9, 2000.
11. London, Coward, McCann & Geoghegan, 1982.
12. December 12, 2000 Supreme Court opinion No. 00–949. Available at <http://www.cnn.com/LAW/library/documents/election.florida/scotus.bush.v.gore.opinion.html>
13. Dowd, 'Liberties; High and low,' *New York Times*, December 3, 2000.
14. Cheney has a history of heart problems. On November 22, 2000, he suffered a 'very slight heart attack.'
15. On August 20, 1998, President Clinton ordered strikes against Afghanistan and Sudan in retaliation for the August 7 bombings of two US embassies in Nairobi, Kenya and Dar es Salaam, Tanzania. On December 16, 1998, Clinton ordered the US armed forces to strike military and security targets in Iraq.
16. In a May 12, 1996 *60 Minutes* interview with Leslie Stahl, Albright responded to the interviewer's question regarding whether she believed the price of over 500,000 dead Iraqi children due to UN sanctions was worth it by saying, 'I think this is a very hard choice, but the price—we think the price is worth it.' Cited in Rahul Mahajan, 'We think the price is worth it; Media uncurious about Iraq's policy effects—there or here,' *FAIR Extra*, November/December 2001. Available online at <http://www.fair.org/extra/0111/iraq.html>

17. Neil Lewis, 'A nation challenged: The detainees; Detentions after attacks pass 1,000, U.S. Says' *New York Times*, October 30, 2001.
18. Revealed at a talk by Eqbal Ahmed at the Transnational Institute (TNI) in Amsterdam, May 1990. Ahmed bought a shoulder-held missile in a market in Islamabad and called a press conference in Pakistan to demonstrate how easily one of these weapons can be acquired.
19. Cited in Charles P. Pierce, 'See Howard run,' *Boston Globe Magazine*, November 24, 2002. Former South Dakota senator and Democratic presidential candidate (1972) George McGovern also cited Aiken's words to Landau as appropriate for Bush just before he ordered US forces to invade Iraq on March 19, 2003.
20. 'The bombshell memo,' *Time Magazine*, June 3, 2002. Edited version of Rowley's memo available online at <http://www.time.com/time/covers/1101020603/memo.html>
21. The late Mel Carnahan was killed in a plane crash on October 16, 2000 just weeks before the election.
22. See <http://www.brainyquote.com/quotes/quotes/h/q125197.html> for Mencken quotes.
23. Molly Ivins, *Fort Worth Star-Telegram*, April 27, 2002.
24. Quoted in my 1972 documentary film, *Robert Wall: Ex-FBI Agent* (available from the Cinema Guild in New York City).
25. *New York Times*, June 3, 2002.
26. The White House press spokesman dismissed the story as 'crap' but Brazilian sources close to President Cardoso like Fernando Pedreira writing in *Estado de Sao Paulo*, April 28, 2002, claimed that the incident actually occurred.
27. Phil Hirschkorn, 'Attention: Padilla's Detention a "constitutional concern,"' *CNN News Online*, June 11, 2002.
28. Cited in Phil Hirschkorn, 'Judge allows lawyers to visit "enemy combatant" a setback for the Bush administration,' *CNN News Online*, March 11, 2003.
29. David Von Drehle, 'GOP victory's ripples spread,' *Washington Post*, November 7, 2002. Extensive Election 2002 coverage available online at <http://www.washingtonpost.com/wp-srv/onpolitics/elections/2002/electionpage.htm>
30. Ibid.
31. John Balzar, 'Crisis is here at home,' *Cincinnati Post*, April 16, 2003.
32. Claire Cozens reports in the November 12, 2002 *Guardian* on TV spending alone: 'New figures show the amount of money spent on TV spots topped £1 bn for the first time, more than double the amount spent on the 1998 mid-term elections.'
33. Story told by the late *Washington Post* reporter Lawrence Stern, 1974.
34. Remark made by Schneider attorney Michael Tigar on the September 9, 2001 broadcast of CBS's *60 Minutes*.
35. The Assistant Secretary of State, William Rogers, affirmed that Kissinger made this remark in a late 1972 background briefing. Several reporters including Stern of the *Washington Post* and Seymour Hersh of the *New York Times* repeated the statement. See the Chile chapter in Hersh, *The Price of Power: Kissinger in the Nixon White House*, Summit Books, 1983.
36. Cited in Lucy Komisar, 'Kissinger declassified,' *The Progressive*, Vol. 63, No. 5, May 1999. Available online at <http://www.progressive.org/komisar9905.htm>
37. Story told by Lawrence Stern, 1976.
38. Cited in 'U.S. endorsed Indonesia's East Timor invasion: Secret documents,' Agence France Presse, December 6, 2001. See Christopher Hitchens, *The Trial of Henry Kissinger*, Verso, 2001, for further discussion on Kissinger's involvement in East Timor.
39. Julian Borger, 'Warden who witnessed 89 executions,' *Guardian*, May 15, 2001.
40. See Abrams' autobiography, *Undue Process: A Story of how Political Differences are Turned into Crimes*, Free Press, 1992.
41. Wade Davis, *Globe and Mail*, July 6, 2002.

42. In the 1950s, Si Kenan founded the American Israel Public Affairs Committee, AIPAC, the United States' largest pro-Israel lobby that continues to work success-fully on securing Congressional military and financial aid to Israel.

43. On February 12, 2003, Belgium's highest court of appeals ruled that Sharon could be tried for war crimes charges only after leaving office. However, on April 1, 2003, Belgium's Lower House in the Parliament voted to effectively water down its contentious universal war crimes law, which previously gave judges the right to hear cases of war crimes committed by anyone and anywhere. According to Andrew Osborn in the April 3, 2003 *Guardian* ('Sharon made safe by Belgian vote on war crime law'), the amended legislation will 'allow those claiming to be the victims of crimes against humanity outside Belgium to bring a case in Belgium only if they have lived there for at least three years,' signaling that Sharon's case will be referred back to Israel and shelved.

44. 'It's the wrong war,' *Gush Shalom*, March 9, 2002.

45. On September 13, 1993, the Palestinian leader, Yasser Arafat, and the Israeli Prime Minister, Yitzhak Rabin, signed the Declaration of Principles, or Oslo Accords, on the White House lawn. Among the provisions of the Oslo Memorandum were the creation of a Palestinian National Authority and future democratic elections; newly recognized Palestinian entities; and the gradual withdrawal of Israeli troops from the Occupied Territories. On September 28, 1995, the Israeli–Palestinian Interim Agreement on the West Bank and Gaza Strip was ratified. Known as Oslo II, this document further detailed the implementation of the second phase of Palestinian self-rule in the Occupied Territories.

46. 'It's the wrong war,' *Gush Shalom*, March 9, 2002.

47. Ellis' remarks made at his October 3, 2001 Campus Forum lecture at Cal Poly Pomona University, Pomona, California.

48. In Brazil, Luis Inacio 'Lula' da Silva of the leftist Workers' Party became President after winning the October 27, 2002 second round of elections; on November 25, 2002, leftist candidate Lucio Gutierrez won the presidential elections in Ecuador; running on an anti-neo-liberal platform, Evo Morales' Movement Toward Socialism (MAS) Party in Bolivia won the second largest bloc of seats after the June 30, 2002 parliamentary elections.

49. Robert B. Zoellick, 'Countering terror with trade,' *Washington Post*, September 20, 2001.

50. The Teapot Dome scandal, named after a rock formation in Wyoming of the same name that hovered over a large government naval oil reserve, stained Warren G. Harding's 1921–23 presidency. The Secretary of the Interior, Albert Fall, a former New Mexico senator and a Harding friend, was convicted of taking bribes from oil executives. Fall received around $400,000 in cash and gifts from oilmen Edward Doheny and Harry Sinclair, who in turn acquired leases to drill for oil reserves at Teapot Dome, Wyoming and Elk Hills, California, respectively. See Phillip Payne, 'What was Teapot Dome?' <http://hnn.us/articles/550.html/>

51. Robert Scheer, 'Enron is a cancer on the presidency,' *Los Angeles Times*, January 2, 2002.

52. Vicente Fox, 'Monterrey: A turning point by Vicente Fox,' *Washington Post*, March 19, 2002.

53. Ibid.

54. Ibid.

55. Cited in Castro's speech at the International Conference on Financing for Development, Monterrey, Mexico, March 21, 2002. Available online at <http://http://www.un.org/ffd/statements/cubaE.htm>

56. Ibid.

57. 'The man guilty of what happened in Monterrey is named Jorge Castañeda,' *Granma*, March 26, 2002.

58. Ibid.

59. Ibid.

60. Ibid.
61. Cited in Castro's speech at the International Conference on Financing for Development, Monterrey, Mexico, March 21, 2002. Available online at <http://www.un.org/ffd/statements/cubaE.htm>
62. Ibid.
63. Ibid.
64. Ibid.
65. On October 19, 2001, Digna Ochoa's body was found in her Mexico City office, with gunshot wounds in the head and arms, apparently from a 22-caliber weapon. Next to her was found a written death threat against members of the Miguel Agustín Pro Human Rights Center, where she had worked to represent victims of human rights abuses, including Mexican environmentalists Rodolfo Montiel and Teodoro Cabrera. As a visible human rights defender in Mexico, Ochoa had faced repeated death threats and was twice kidnapped in 1999. See Angel Bolaños and Andrea Becerril, 'Human rights defender Digna Ochoa assassinated in her office,' La Jornada, October 20, 2001; the Sierra Club's June 2002 update on Ochoa, <http://www.sierraclub.org/human-rights/Mexico/ochoa.asp>
66. The quotations in this chapter and the following one are from interviews which I conducted while filming scenes in Juarez for Maquila: A Tale of Two Mexicos (2000, distributed by Cinema Guild, NYC and shown on Worldlink TV) or for my forthcoming documentary, We Don't Play Golf Here, on the border and the environment.
67. Since 9/11, armed civilian groups unofficially patrolling the US–Mexican border have emerged in Arizona under the guise of 'spotting illegals and terrorists,' according to a member of the Civil Homeland Defense, founded in the border town of Tombstone. Other Arizona-based vigilante groups include Ranch Rescue and American Border Patrol. See Julie Watson, 'Armed civilians watch for Mexican border crossers,' Associated Press, February 8, 2003.
68. John Dinges and Saul Landau, Assassination on Embassy Row, Pantheon Books, 1980, pp. 237–9.
69. Ibid., pp. 238–9.
70. Ibid., p. 239.
71. Mills relayed this story to me in December 1960.
72. Cited in Duncan Campbell, 'The Bush dynasty and the Cuban criminals,' Guardian, December 2, 2002.
73. Cited in Howard Wilkinson, 'Bush: "We refuse to live in fear,"' Cincinnati Enquirer, October 8, 2002.
74. Cited in Raymond Williams, Communications, Pelican, 1982, p. 26.
75. Cited in La Jornada, April 12, 2002.
76. Julia Sweig, Inside the Cuban Revolution, Harvard University Press, 2002.
77. Broadcast on CNN's Crossfire, September 27, 2002.
78. Cited in Lobe's 'Chicken Hawks as Cheer Leaders,' Project Against the Present Danger, September 6, 2002.
79. Nickles made the statement on ABC TV's This Week. Cited in Joyce Howard Price, 'Democrats blast US line on Iraq,' Washington Times, September 30, 2002.
80. During President Bush's January 29, 2002 State of the Union address, he singled out North Korea, Iran and Iraq as states constituting 'an axis of evil, arming to threaten the peace of the world,' generating immediate criticism from both the cited governments and US allies alike. David Frum, a former member of the Bush speech-writing team, is credited with coining the controversial phrase. See text of Address at <http://www.whitehouse.gov/news/releases/2002/01/20020129-11.html>
81. Cited in Robert Windrem, 'Rumsfeld key player in Iraq policy shift,' MSNBC, August 18, 2002.
82. Ibid.
83. 'Confrontation in the Gulf: Excerpts from Iraqi document on meeting with US envoy,' New York Times, September 23, 1990.

84. Mentioned in Thomas W. Lippman and Barton Gellman, 'US says it collected Iraq intelligence via UNSCOM,' *Washington Post*, January 8, 1999.

85. Sartre quote available online at <http://www.quoteworld.org/browse.php?thetext= milit,war,army,navy&page=19>

86. These CIA quotations are from the CIA Director George J. Tenet's 'Letter to Senate on Baghdad's intentions,' October 7, 2002, sent to Bob Graham (Democrat–Florida), the former chairman of the Senate's Intelligence Committee. Available on the Education for Peace in Iraq Center's web site at <http:/epic-usa.org/resources/ rpt.php?n=03#letter>

87. Bush was speaking at the Cincinnati Museum Center, Ohio. Speech available online at <http://www.whitehouse.gov/news/releases/2002/10/20021007-8.html>

88. Powell, speaking on February 14, 2003 to the UN Security Council. Speech available online at <http://www.state.gov/secretary/rm/2003/17763.htm>

89. 'Memorandum for the President, from: Veteran Intelligence Professionals for Sanity, CommonDreams.org, February 7, 2003. Available online at <http:// www.common- dreams.org/views03/0207-04.htm>

90. Cited in Matthew Tempest, 'Kaufman: MPs won't support Iraq attack,' *Guardian*, August 15, 2002.

91. Koza's memo is available online on the *Guardian* web site at <http:// observer.guardian.co.uk/iraq/story/0,12239,905954,00.html>

92. Available online at <http://www.etsu.edu/cas/history/docs/lodgeagainst.htm>

93. Borah's speech is available online at <http://www.mutied.com/documents. Borah.html>

94. Cited in Agee's August 1975 *Playboy* interview. See his book *CIA Diary: Inside the Company*, Penguin Books, 1975.

95. Cited in Justice Jackson's 'Statement on War Trials Agreement', August 12, 1945. Available online at Yale University's Avalon Project, <http://www.yale.edu/lawweb/ avalon/imt/jack02.htm>

96. Cited in Dana Priest and Karen DeYoung, 'CIA questioned documents linking Iraq, Uranium Ore', *Washington Post*, March 22, 2003.

97. Cited in the September 2002 'National Security Strategy of the United States of America.' Available online at <http://www.whitehouse.gov/nsc/nss.pdf>

98. Conclusion of Mario Savio's December 3, 1964 Berkeley, California speech before the Free Speech Movement sit-in. Available online at <http://www.fsm-a.org/stacks/ mario/mario_speech.html>

99. Quoted by Coretta Scott King, January 19, 2003, at the Ebenezer Baptist Church, Atlanta, Georgia.

100. President Bush's remarks released by the White House Office of the Press Secretary, August 29, 2002.

101. In response to a reporter's question at the White House on February 18, 2003, Bush said about the anti-war demonstrations in the US and abroad, 'Size of protest—it's like deciding, well, I'm going to decide policy based upon a focus group.' Cited in Richard Stevenson, 'Ten Million People is "Focus Group,"' *New York Times*, February 19, 2003.

102. 'Iraqis have paid the blood price for a fraudulent war', *Guardian*, April 10, 2003.

103. Cited in Emma Goldman's speech, 'The tragedy of woman's emancipation.' Available at <http://www.identitytheory.com/etexts/goldmananarchism11.html>

104. NLF stood for National Liberation Front, tied to the communist government of North Vietnam. This chant expressed anti-Vietnam War protestors' support for the Vietnamese resistance and was popular at rallies.

105. Cited in Kate Linker, *Love for Sale: The Words and Pictures of Barbara Kruger*, Harry N. Abrams Inc., 1990, p. 64.

106. Ibid. p. 76.

107. Ibid. p. 28.

Bibliography

BOOKS

Tariq Ali, *The Clash of Fundamentalisms: Crusades, Jihads and Modernity*, Verso Books, 2002, and Ahmed Rashid, *Taliban*, Yale University Press, 2001; *Jihad*, Yale University Press/World Policy Institute, 2002. These books together provide an immense amount of factual and analytical material on a key, but less than studied area of conflict.

Sarah Anderson and John Cavanagh, *Field Guide to the Global Economy*, The New Press, 2000. This book will provide those without background with the necessary tools to explore the issues around the global economy. It is a great compendium of facts and sources.

Walden Bello, *Dark Victory: The United States and Global Poverty*, TNI/Food First/Pluto Press, 1999. An excellent analysis of how US policy not only conflicts with aspirations of Third World peoples, but vitiates their needs as well.

Phyllis Bennis, *Before and After: US Foreign Policy and the September 11th Crisis*, Interlink Publishing Group, 2002. An insightful critique of US policy, before and after the 9/11 happenings.

Noam Chomsky: *9/11*, Seven Stories Press, 2001.

Susan George, *The Lugano Report: On Preserving Capitalism in the 21st Century*, Pluto Press, 1999. This book makes key arguments about the nature of corporate globalization.

Tom Hayden (ed.), *The Zapatista Reader*, Nation Books, 2002. This book gives readers much of what they need to know and then some on the struggle in Chiapas and the revolt of indigenous people.

Seymour Hersh, *The Price of Power: Kissinger in the Nixon White House*, Summit Books, 1983.

Christopher Hitchens, *The Trial of Henry Kissinger*, Verso, 2001. Hitchens writes a literary indictment of the former national security adviser and secretary of state to presidents Nixon and Ford, especially regarding his policies on Indonesia (E. Timor), Vietnam and Chile and Cambodia.

Arianna Huffington, *Pigs at the Trough: How Corporate Greed and Political Corruption are Undermining America*, Crown, 2003. Huffington shows how capitalism really works.

Chalmers Johnson, *Blowback: The Cost and Consequences of American Empire*, Henry Holt, 2000. Johnson writes about how failure to measure consequences of US policies has resulted in 'blowback' (a CIA term that signifies the client has turned against his employer). Johnson suggests that the 9/11 events might well belong in this category.

Arundhati Roy, *Power Politics*, South End Books, 2001. A formidable writer with immense courage.

Edward W. Said, *Reflections on Exile and Other Essays*, Harvard University Press, 2002. A man of great wisdom.

Tom Segev (ed.), *The Other Israel: Voices of Refusal and Dissent*, New Press, 2002. Especially interesting in the essay by Uri Avnery.

Julia Sweig, *Inside the Cuban Revolution*, Harvard University Press, 2002. This book provides rare insights into the political origins of Cuba's revolution. It uses previously classified documents from Cuba's Council of State archive to show how Fidel Castro interacted with rivals and allies in the politics of the insurrection, 1957–58.

Gore Vidal, *Perpetual War for Perpetual Peace?*, Nation Books, 2002; *Dreaming War: Blood for Oil and the Cheney-Bush Junta*, Nation Books, 2002. Vidal, not only one of the great historians (see his many novels), has set forth a trenchant critique of imperial designs and the narrow-minded elite who manage the empire.

Howard Zinn, *Terrorism and War*, Seven Stories Press, 2002. One of the great living historians.

Stephen Zunes, *Tinderbox: US Middle East Policy and the Roots of Terrorism*, Common Courage Press, 2003. Cogent analysis.

WEB SITES

Progreso Weekly: <http://www.rprogreso.com>
CounterPunch: <http://www.counterpunch.org>
Tom Paine: <http://www.tompaine.com>
Not in Our Name: <http://www.notinourname.net>
Common Dreams: <http://www.commondreams.org>
Z Mag: <http://www.zmag.org>
Antiterroristas.cu: <http://www.antiterroristas.cu>
Institute for Policy Studies (IPS): <http://www.ips-dc.org>
Transnational Institute (TNI): <http://www.tni.org>

Index